Covenant
and
Communion

Covenant *and* Communion

The Biblical Theology *of* Pope Benedict XVI

Scott W. Hahn

BrazosPress

a division of Baker Publishing Group
Grand Rapids, Michigan

© 2009 by Scott W. Hahn

Published by Brazos Press
a division of Baker Publishing Group
P.O. Box 6287, Grand Rapids, MI 49516-6287
www.brazospress.com

Printed in the United States of America

Library of Congress Cataloging-in-Publication Data

Hahn, Scott.
    Covenant and communion : the biblical theology of Pope Benedict XVI /
Scott W. Hahn.
        p.   cm.
    Includes bibliographical references and indexes.
    ISBN 978-1-58743-269-9 (cloth)
    1. Benedict XVI, Pope, 1927– 2. Theology. 3. Catholic Church—Doctrines. I. Title.
BX1378.6.H34 2009
230′.041092—dc22   2009018847

Dedicated to
Pope Benedict XVI,
holy father

We have to enter into a relationship of awe and obedience toward the Bible, which nowadays is frequently in danger of being lost.

Pope Benedict XVI

Contents

Abbreviations   9

1. Ignorance of Scripture Is Ignorance of Christ:
   The Theological Project of Joseph Ratzinger   13

2. The Critique of Criticism: Beginning the Search for a New
   Theological Synthesis   25

3. The Hermeneutic of Faith: Critical and Historical
   Foundations for a Biblical Theology   41

4. The Spiritual Science of Theology: Its Mission and Method
   in the Life of the Church   63

5. Reading God's Testament to Humankind: Biblical Realism,
   Typology, and the Inner Unity of Revelation   91

6. The Theology of the Divine Economy: Covenant,
   Kingdom, and the History of Salvation   115

7. The Embrace of Salvation: Mystagogy and the
   Transformation of Sacrifice   137

8. The Cosmic Liturgy: The Eucharistic Kingdom and the World as Temple   163

9. The Authority of Mystery: The Beauty and Necessity of the Theologian's Task   187

Scripture Index   197

Subject Index   199

Abbreviations

Unless otherwise noted, all documents of Benedict's pontificate can be found at www.vatican.va/holy_father/benedict_xvi/index.htm. The following abbreviations are used for the works of Joseph Cardinal Ratzinger / Pope Benedict XVI that are frequently cited. When available, the original publication date appears in parentheses next to the publication date of the English translation.

Beginning	Cardinal Joseph Ratzinger. *In the Beginning: A Catholic Understanding of the Story of Creation and the Fall.* Translated by Boniface Ramsey. Grand Rapids: Eerdmans, 1995 (1986).
Benedict XVI	John F. Thornton and Susan B. Varenne, eds. *The Essential Pope Benedict XVI: His Central Writings and Speeches.* San Francisco: HarperSanFrancisco, 2007.
Catechism	Joseph Cardinal Ratzinger. *Gospel, Catechesis, Catechism: Sidelights on* The Catechism of the Catholic Church. San Francisco: Ignatius, 1997 (1995).
Communion	Joseph Cardinal Ratzinger. *Called to Communion: Understanding the Church Today.* Translated by Adrian Walker. San Francisco: Ignatius, 1996 (1991).
Co-Workers	Joseph Cardinal Ratzinger. *Co-Workers of the Truth: Meditations for Every Day of the Year.* Edited by Irene Grassl. Translated by Mary Frances McCarthy and Lothar Krauth. San Francisco: Ignatius, 1992.

Dogma	Joseph Ratzinger. *Dogma and Preaching*. Translated by Matthew J. O'Connell. Chicago: Franciscan Herald, 1985 (1973).
Ecumenism	Joseph Ratzinger. *Church, Ecumenism, and Politics: New Essays in Ecclesiology*. New York: Crossroad, 1988 (1987).
Eschatology	Joseph Ratzinger. *Eschatology: Death and Eternal Life*. Translated by Michael Waldstein. Washington, DC: Catholic University of America Press, 1988 (1977).
Eucharist	Joseph Cardinal Ratzinger. *God Is Near Us: The Eucharist, the Heart of Life*. Edited by Stephen Otto Horn and Vinzenz Pfnür. Translated by Henry Taylor. San Francisco: Ignatius, 2003 (2001).
Faith	Joseph Cardinal Ratzinger. *Feast of Faith: Approaches to a Theology of the Liturgy*. Translated by Graham Harrison. San Francisco: Ignatius, 1986 (1981).
"Interpretation"	Joseph Cardinal Ratzinger. "Biblical Interpretation in Crisis." In *The Essential Pope Benedict XVI: His Central Writings and Speeches*. Edited by John F. Thornton and Susan B. Varenne, 243–58. San Francisco: HarperSanFrancisco, 2007.
Jesus	Pope Benedict XVI. *Jesus of Nazareth: From the Baptism in the Jordan to the Transfiguration*. Translated by Adrian J. Walker. New York: Doubleday, 2007.
Liturgy	Joseph Cardinal Ratzinger. *The Spirit of the Liturgy*. Translated by John Saward. San Francisco: Ignatius, 2000.
"Magisterium"	Joseph Cardinal Ratzinger. "Relationship between Magisterium and Exegetes." Address to the Pontifical Biblical Commission. In *L'Osservatore Romano*. Weekly Edition in English. July 23, 2003.
Pierced	Joseph Cardinal Ratzinger. *Behold the Pierced One: An Approach to a Spiritual Christology*. Translated by Graham Harrison. San Francisco: Ignatius, 1986 (1984).

Pilgrim	Joseph Cardinal Ratzinger. *Pilgrim Fellowship of Faith: The Church as Communion*. Edited by Stephan Otto Horn and Vinzenz Pfnür. Translated by Henry Taylor. San Francisco: Ignatius, 2005 (2002).
"Preface"	Joseph Cardinal Ratzinger. "Preface." In *The Jewish People and Their Sacred Scriptures in the Christian Bible*, 11–19. Pontifical Biblical Commission. Boston: Pauline Books and Media, 2003.
"Primacy"	Joseph Ratzinger. "Primacy, Episcopate, and Apostolic Succession." In *The Episcopate and the Primacy*, 37–63. Karl Rahner and Joseph Ratzinger. New York: Herder and Herder, 1962.
Principles	Joseph Cardinal Ratzinger. *Principles of Catholic Theology: Building Stones for a Fundamental Theology*. Translated by Mary Frances McCarthy. San Francisco: Ignatius, 1987 (1982).
Religions	Joseph Cardinal Ratzinger. *Many Religions, One Covenant: Israel, the Church, and the World*. Translated by Graham Harrison. San Francisco: Ignatius, 1999 (1998).
"Revelation"	Joseph Ratzinger. "Revelation and Tradition." In *Revelation and Tradition*, 26–49. Karl Rahner and Joseph Ratzinger. New York: Herder and Herder, 1966.
Song	Joseph Cardinal Ratzinger. *A New Song for the Lord: Faith in Christ and Liturgy Today*. Translated by Martha M. Matesich. New York: Crossroad, 1996 (1995).
Theology	Joseph Cardinal Ratzinger. *The Nature and Mission of Theology: Approaches to Understanding Its Role in the Light of Present Controversy*. Translated by Adrian Walker. San Francisco: Ignatius, 1995 (1993).
Truth	Joseph Cardinal Ratzinger. *Truth and Tolerance: Christian Belief and World Religions*. Translated by Henry Taylor. San Francisco: Ignatius, 2004 (2003).
Way	Pope Benedict XVI. *On the Way to Jesus Christ*. Translated by Michael Miller. San Francisco: Ignatius, 2005 (2004).

1

Ignorance of Scripture Is Ignorance of Christ

The Theological Project of Joseph Ratzinger

The Most Urgent Priority

Never before in the history of the Catholic Church has a world-class biblical theologian been elevated to the papacy. Joseph Cardinal Ratzinger's election on April 19, 2005, brought to the Chair of St. Peter one of the world's finest theological minds. He was a public intellectual long engaged in dialogue concerning the crucial issues of the modern period, especially the crucial relationships between faith and reason, freedom and truth, and history and dogma.

The pontificate of Pope Benedict XVI, to a degree not seen perhaps since the medieval papacy of Gregory the Great, has borne the stamp of a distinctive biblical theology. There is an intensely biblical quality to his pastoral teaching, and he has demonstrated a keen concern for the authentic interpretation of sacred Scripture.

For Benedict, the Church lives, moves, and takes its being from the Word of God—through whom all things were created in the beginning, through whom the face of God was revealed in the flesh of Jesus Christ, and through whom God's new covenant is witnessed to in the inspired texts of Scripture and made present in the divine liturgy.

Benedict's command of the biblical texts, the patristic interpretative tradition, and the findings of historical and literary scholarship represents the full flowering of the Catholic biblical renewal that culminated in *Dei Verbum*, the Second Vatican Council's constitution on divine revelation.[1] As a young theologian, Ratzinger himself had a hand in drafting that Vatican II document. If the first half of the twentieth century was marked by the *emergence* of three renewal movements—the biblical, the patristic, and the liturgical—then we see the *convergence* of these movements in *Dei Verbum*. And in the theology of Benedict we see their integration and coordination.

More than any other theologian in his time, Benedict has articulated a biblical theology that synthesizes modern scientific methods with the theological hermeneutic of spiritual exegesis that began in the New Testament writers and patristic commentators and has continued throughout the Church's tradition. In fact, there has been no other Catholic theologian in the last century, if ever, whose theology is as highly developed and integrated in explicitly biblical terms.

Yet these facts have gone largely unnoticed in the growing body of secondary literature on Benedict's theological thought and vision. Benedict himself has identified his theology as having a "biblical character."[2] Nonetheless, even the best of these recent studies pays little if any attention to this dimension of his work.[3] When in early 2007 he published *Jesus of Nazareth*, the first of a

1. For a historical perspective, see Joseph G. Prior, *The Historical Critical Method in Catholic Exegesis*, Tesi Gregoriana Serie Teologia 50 (Rome: Pontifical Gregorian University, 1999).

2. Joseph Cardinal Ratzinger with Peter Seewald, *Salt of the Earth: Christianity and the Catholic Church at the End of the Millennium*, trans. Adrian Walker (San Francisco: Ignatius, 1997), 66.

3. See, for instance, these important scholarly studies: Maximilian Heinrich Heim, *Joseph Ratzinger: Life in the Church and Living Theology*, trans. Michael J. Miller (San Francisco: Ignatius, 2007); Tracey Rowland, *Ratzinger's Faith: The Theology of Pope Benedict XVI* (New York: Oxford University Press, 2008). While valuable in many respects, neither of these works engages the foundations of Benedict's theological vision in his interpretation of Scripture.

projected two-volume work of spiritual Christology, many were genuinely surprised at the note of urgency sounded by the eighty-year-old pontiff:

> Since my election to the episcopal see of Rome I have used every free moment to make progress on the book. As I do not know how much more time or strength I am still to be given, I have decided to publish the first ten chapters . . . because it struck me as the most urgent priority to present the figure and message of Jesus in his public ministry, and so to help foster the growth of a living relationship with him.[4]

Jesus of Nazareth is a significant contribution to biblical Christology and a deep expression of Benedict's theological vision. To those of us who have been studying Benedict closely for many years now, *Jesus of Nazareth* came not as a curious surprise but as a fitting dénouement. It is the culmination of his theological method, pastoral concerns, and ardent sense of the needs of the hour in the Church.

That is why I have written this essay. I have had the privilege of introducing two of Joseph Ratzinger's works to the English-speaking world,[5] and in recent years I have grown increasingly aware of how profoundly my own work has been influenced by my encounter with his thinking over a quarter of a century. In the pages that follow, I hope to offer an appreciation of how and why Benedict engages in theology and biblical interpretation. I also hope to present a kind of synthesis of his work, suggesting the main outlines of his biblical theology. I write as a professional theologian and exegete and as one who believes that Benedict's vision has much to teach those of us in this privileged guild. His is a theology of great power and beauty.

I stress that what I offer here is an *essay*. In these pages I want to listen to Benedict, to follow his patterns of thought, and to carefully attend to his priorities and concerns. I want to allow him to speak

---

4. *Jesus*, xxiv.
5. See my forewords to *Religions* and Joseph Cardinal Ratzinger, *The Meaning of Christian Brotherhood* (San Francisco: Ignatius, 1993 [1960]).

as much as possible, which is why what follows might be called an exercise in explanatory theology. In some places I have had to resist the temptation to present a simple catena of his thoughts. While I have resisted that temptation, I have still tried to assist in the presentation of Benedict's own ideas, not simply advance my own understandings of these issues.

This is not, then, a treatise or a dissertation. Such works will need to be written on the many facets of Benedict's wide-ranging theological project. But before that work can be done adequately, I believe that we need to understand the foundations of his project, which rest in his approach to and appropriation of sacred Scripture.

Benedict is less a systematic thinker than he is a symphonic thinker. This essay will undoubtedly reflect that. His writings show a cast of mind that is more comparable to that of the Church Fathers than to that of traditional dogmatic and systematic theologians such as Thomas Aquinas or Matthias Scheeben. In the Fathers we find the notion that truth consists of a unity of diverse elements, much as a symphony brings into a single, harmonious whole the music played on a variety of instruments. This is how it is with the biblical theology of Benedict. Even his occasional writings, which make up the bulk of his oeuvre, are usually composed like a polyphonic melody from many differentiated strains—scriptural, historical, literary, liturgical, and patristic.

A Brief Theological and Ecclesial Résumé

The former Joseph Ratzinger was a young academic theologian with a very bright future when, in 1977, he was chosen to be arch-bishop of the historic Bavarian diocese of Munich and Freising. He took for his episcopal motto a biblical expression: "coopera-tors in the truth" (3 John 8). This phrase expressed his sense of the continuity between his theological work and his new service in the administrative hierarchy of the Church.

Despite all the differences in modality, what is involved was and remains the same: to follow the truth, to be at its service. And, because in today's world the theme of truth has all but disappeared, because truth appears to be too great for man and yet everything falls apart if there is no truth; for these reasons, this motto also seemed timely in the good sense of the word.[6]

In practical terms, however, his election to the episcopacy brought to an end his promising career as an academic theologian. He would seldom again have the opportunity for sustained scholarly research and writing, a situation about which he still occasionally expresses regret. Writing of his calling to Munich, he noted: "I felt that . . . at this period of my life—I was fifty years old—I had found my own theological vision and could now create an *oeuvre* with which I would contribute something to the whole of theology."[7]

In forewords or afterwords to his books, he sometimes expresses disappointment that his professional obligations have made it impossible to develop his ideas with the depth and precision he would like.[8] Nonetheless, in the last quarter-century, Benedict has produced a substantial body of biblical-theological work, including books, articles, speeches, and homilies. This work reflects the wide range of his study and interests and the keen, symphonic turn of his mind. Close study of this body of writings suggests that, had professor Ratzinger been left alone to pursue his scholarly passions, his achievements would have rivaled or surpassed those of the greatest Catholic theologians of the last century—figures such as Hans Urs von Balthasar and Karl Rahner. His *Opera Omnia* are expected to fill sixteen volumes, indicating the scope of his interests and the breadth of his accomplishments.[9]

6. Joseph Cardinal Ratzinger, *Milestones: Memoirs, 1927–1977*, trans. Erasmo Leiva-Merkiakis (San Francisco: Ignatius, 1998), 153.

7. Ratzinger with Seewald, *Salt*, 81.

8. See, for example, *Theology*, 8; *Religions*, 19.

9. Publication of Benedict's collected works began in 2008 by the German publisher Herder and the Vatican's Libreria Editrice Vaticana. As announced, the opera will include: vols. 1–2: his undergraduate and doctorate theses and other writings about Augustine and Bonaventure, the subjects of those theses; vol. 3: his inaugural lecture, "The God of Faith and the God of the Philosophers," delivered at Bonn in 1959, and other writings on faith and reason and the historical and intellectual foundations of Europe; vol. 4: *Introduction to Christianity* (1968) and other writings on the profession of faith, baptism, discipleship, and Christian life;

It is beyond the scope of the present book to provide a complete résumé of Benedict's career, but I should note a few highlights.[10] He received his doctorate in theology from the University of Munich in 1953, writing his dissertation on Augustine's exegesis and ecclesiology. He lectured in fundamental theology at several German universities before assuming the chair in dogmatic theology at the University of Tübingen in 1966. He was an expert theological *peritus*, or adviser, at the Second Vatican Council (1963–65) and, as I noted above, made important contributions to the council's pivotal document on divine revelation, *Dei Verbum*.[11] In addition to hundreds of articles published in academic and ecclesial journals, he is the author of books of enduring importance and influence on the nature and mission of theology,[12] patristic theology and exegesis,[13] ecclesiology,[14] liturgical theology,[15] dogmatic theology,[16]

vol. 5: writings on creation, anthropology, the doctrine of grace, and Mariology; vol. 6: works on Christology, including *Jesus of Nazareth* (2007); vol. 7: writings on Vatican Council II, including notes and comments from that period; vol. 8: writings on ecclesiology and ecumenism; vol. 9: writings on theological epistemology and hermeneutics, specifically on the understanding of Scripture, revelation, and tradition; vol. 10: *Eschatology* (1977) and other writings on hope, death, resurrection, and eternal life; vol. 11: writings on the theology of the liturgy; vol. 12: writings on the sacraments and ministry; vol. 13: collected interviews; vol. 14: homilies from before his election as pope; vol. 15: autobiographical and personal writings; vol. 16: complete bibliography and comprehensive index of all the volumes. See Sandro Magister, "In the 'Opera Omnia' of Ratzinger the Theologian, the Overture Is All about the Liturgy," available at http://chiesa.espresso.repubblica.it/articolo/208933?eng=y.

10. For a good overview, especially of his early academic writings, see Aidan Nichols, *The Thought of Benedict XVI: An Introduction to the Theology of Joseph Ratzinger* (London: Burns & Oates, 2005). For comprehensive bibliographies, see Nichols, *Thought of Benedict XVI*, 297–330; Heim, *Joseph Ratzinger*, 539–63; *Pilgrim*, 299–379.

11. For an excellent window into his work at the Second Vatican Council, see Jared Wicks, "Six Texts by Prof. Joseph Ratzinger as *Peritus* before and during Vatican Council II," *Gregorianum* 89, no. 2 (2008): 233–311. See also Ratzinger, *Milestones*, 120–31.

12. See *Theology* and *Principles*.

13. See Joseph Ratzinger, *The Theology of History in St. Bonaventure*, trans. Zachary Hayes (Chicago: Franciscan Herald, 1971).

14. See *The Meaning of Christian Brotherhood*.

15. See *Liturgy*.

16. See *Eschatology*.

the Christian symbol of faith,[17] and Christology.[18] And in collaboration with some of last century's most influential theologians, including Henri de Lubac and Hans Urs von Balthasar, he cofounded the important theological journal *Communio*.

As the highest ranking doctrinal official in the Catholic Church for nearly twenty years, he helped oversee the teaching of the faith in Catholic universities and seminaries throughout the world and played an important role in the work of the International Theological Commission and the Pontifical Biblical Commission. He was also a decisive intellectual force in the development of the *Catechism of the Catholic Church*, the first comprehensive statement of Catholic belief and practice to be published in more than four hundred and fifty years. Reflecting his clear priorities, Benedict has said of the *Catechism*: "As far as I know, there has never been until now a catechism so thoroughly formed by the Bible."[19]

The Crisis of Faith in Christ

Benedict's theological training and career were shaped by his encounter with the historical-critical method of biblical interpretation, which by the late 1940s had become the dominant theoretical model in the academy.[20] In autobiographical reflections, he has related how confident scholars were at that time that the method gave them "the last word" on the meaning of biblical texts. He relates a story about a leading Tübingen exegete who announced he would no longer entertain dissertation proposals because "everything in the New Testament had already been researched."[21]

Well schooled in its techniques and findings, Benedict has nonetheless emerged as a forceful critic of what he describes as the theoretical hubris and practical limitations of historical criticism. For him, the issues involved are far from merely academic. Indeed,

17. See Joseph Cardinal Ratzinger, *Introduction to Christianity*, trans. J. R. Foster (San Francisco: Ignatius, 1990 [1968]).
18. See *Jesus*.
19. *Catechism*, 61; see also 65n24.
20. *Eschatology*, 271–72.
21. *Pilgrim*, 27.

the stakes in the debate could hardly be higher. How we read and interpret the Bible directly affects what we believe about Christ, the Church, the sacraments, and the liturgy.[22]

Benedict knows and often quotes the solemn truth expressed memorably by St. Jerome: "Ignorance of the Scriptures is ignorance of Christ."[23] He has gone so far as to suggest that a near-exclusive reliance on the historical-critical method has resulted in widespread ignorance about the true nature, identity, and mission of Christ. Referring to the method, he writes: "The crisis of faith in Christ in recent times began with a modified way of reading sacred Scripture—seemingly the sole scientific way."[24]

As we will see in the chapters that follow, for Benedict an exclusive reliance on historical-critical methods has resulted in a diminishment or reduction in the figure of Jesus, who is no longer believed to be the "Lord" or the Son of God but is considered to be simply "a man who is nothing more than the advocate of all men." This viewpoint, he adds, "has emphatically impressed itself on the public consciousness and has made major inroads into the congregations of Christian believers in all churches."[25]

This concern for the distortion in the image of Jesus forms the wider context for *Jesus of Nazareth* and explains the sense of urgency Benedict felt about its publication. It also explains why he took the unprecedented step of devoting a key passage to the

22. See *Song*, 30: "The historical Jesus can only be a non-Christ, a non-Son [of God]. . . . As a result, the Church falls apart all by herself; now she can only be an organization made by humans that tries, more or less skillfully and more or less benevolently, to put this Jesus to use. The sacraments, of course, fall by the wayside—how could there be a real presence of this 'historical Jesus' in the Eucharist?"

23. Jerome, *Commentary on Isaiah 1:1*, quoted in Second Vatican Council, *Dei Verbum*, Dogmatic Constitution on Divine Revelation (November 18, 1965), 25, in *The Scripture Documents: An Anthology of Official Catholic Teachings*, ed. Dean P. Béchard, SJ (Collegeville, MN: Liturgical Press, 2002), 30. For an example of Benedict's use of Jerome, see his "Address to the Participants in the International Congress Organized to Commemorate the Fortieth Anniversary of the Dogmatic Constitution on Divine Revelation, *Dei Verbum*" (September 16, 2005), in *L'Osservatore Romano*, Weekly Edition in English (September 21, 2005), 7. As pope, Benedict has devoted two public teachings to Jerome. See the General Audiences of November 7 and November 14, 2007.

24. *Way*, 9.

25. *Way*, 8; see also 61–62.

issues of biblical interpretation in the Church in his inaugural homily as Bishop of Rome. Echoing many of the concerns and preoccupations of his theological career, Benedict stated:

> In the Church, Sacred Scripture, the understanding of which increases under the inspiration of the Holy Spirit, and the ministry of its authentic interpretation that was conferred upon the Apostles, are indissolubly bound.
>
> Whenever Sacred Scripture is separated from the living voice of the Church, it falls prey to disputes among experts. Of course, all they have to tell us is important and invaluable; the work of scholars is a considerable help in understanding the living process in which the Scriptures developed, hence, also in grasping their historical richness.
>
> Yet science alone cannot provide us with a definitive and binding interpretation; it is unable to offer us, in its interpretation, that certainty with which we can live and for which we can even die. A greater mandate is necessary for this, which cannot derive from human abilities alone. The voice of the living Church is essential for this, of the Church entrusted until the end of time to Peter and to the College of the Apostles.
>
> This power of teaching frightens many people in and outside the Church. They wonder whether freedom of conscience is threatened or whether it is a presumption opposed to freedom of thought. It is not like this. The power that Christ conferred upon Peter and his Successors is, in an absolute sense, a mandate to serve. The power of teaching in the Church involves a commitment to the service of obedience to the faith.
>
> The Pope is not an absolute monarch whose thoughts and desires are law. On the contrary: the Pope's ministry is a guarantee of obedience to Christ and to his Word. He must not proclaim his own ideas, but rather constantly bind himself and the Church to obedience to God's Word, in the face of every attempt to adapt it or water it down, and every form of opportunism.[26]

---

26. Pope Benedict XVI, Homily, Mass of Possession of the Chair of the Bishop of Rome (May 7, 2005), in *L'Osservatore Romano*, Weekly Edition in English (May 11, 2005), 3. Frequently in his teaching, Benedict appears to be in "dialogue" with the ideas of influential exegetes, sometimes even referring to them by name. See, for example, his criticism of Adolf von Harnack and the "the individualism of liberal theology"

These are most unusual words for a papal homily, but these are unusual times in the Church. That Benedict chose these words in setting out the vision for his pontificate tells us a great deal about his theology. In a sense, the present essay will be an unfolding of these words.

While Benedict has spoken of "the authority of mystery"[27] in the context of the liturgy, this expression is also helpful for describing his integral vision of the Church as the handmaiden of the Word of God. The Church, as he sees it, lives under the authority of mystery. It is in dialogue with the Word that revealed the mystery of God's saving plan in history, and it is in obedient service to the Word as it seeks final accomplishment of God's plan.

Benedict has a bold understanding of the mystery of the Word in history and in the human heart. As I write, he has just finished presiding over a Synod of Bishops that brought to Rome more than two hundred and fifty bishops from around the world. For nearly a month they met daily from morning to night to discuss a topic personally chosen by Benedict, "The Word of God in the Life and Mission of the Church." To open the Synod, Benedict offered a beautiful meditation on Psalm 118 in which he laid out his vision in terms that can only be described as breathtaking. His words reflect a lifetime of contemplation and anticipate the themes we are about to study:

> Humanly speaking, the word, my human word, is almost nothing in reality, a breath. As soon as it is pronounced it disappears. It seems to be nothing. But already the human word has incredible power. Words create history, words form thoughts, the thoughts that create the word. It is the word that forms history, reality.
>
> Furthermore, the Word of God is the foundation of everything, it is the true reality. . . . Therefore, we must change our concept of realism. The realist is the one who recognizes the Word of God, in this apparently weak reality, as the foundation of all things. . . .
>
> All things come from the Word, they are products of the Word. "In the beginning was the Word." In the beginning the heavens spoke. And thus reality was born of the Word, it is *creatura Verbi*.

---

made during the course of his General Audience (March 15, 2006), in *L'Osservatore Romano*, Weekly Edition in English (March 22, 2006), 11.

27. *Song*, 32.

All is created from the Word and all is called to serve the Word. This means that all of creation, in the end, is conceived of to create the place of encounter between God and his creature—a place where the history of love between God and his creature can develop. . . . The history of salvation is not a small event, on a poor planet, in the immensity of the universe. It is not a minimal thing which happens by chance on a lost planet. It is the motive for everything, the motive for creation. Everything is created so that this story can exist—the encounter between God and his creature. In this sense, salvation history, the covenant, precedes creation. During the Hellenistic period, Judaism developed the idea that the *Torah* would have preceded the creation of the material world. This material world seems to have been created solely to make room for the *Torah*, for this Word of God that creates the answer and becomes the history of love. The mystery of Christ already is mysteriously revealed here. This is what we are told in the Letter to the Ephesians and to the Colossians: Christ is the *protòtypos*, the first-born of creation, the idea for which the universe was conceived. He welcomes all. We enter in the movement of the universe by uniting with Christ. One can say that, while material creation is the condition for the history of salvation, the history of the covenant is the true cause of the cosmos. We reach the roots of being by reaching the mystery of Christ, his living Word that is the aim of all creation. In serving the Lord we achieve the purpose of being, the purpose of our own existence.[28]

In his biography of Benedict's predecessor, George Weigel suggested that Pope John Paul II's "theology of the body" would be his greatest legacy to the Church. Weigel described John Paul's theology as "a kind of theological time bomb set to go off with dramatic consequences" for theology, preaching, religious education, and even our understanding of the Creed.[29] This is a bold claim indeed, and one I believe may prove to be accurate. But I also believe a similar claim can be made for the biblical theology of Pope Benedict. It is a theology in which can be seen the essential

28. Pope Benedict XVI, Meditation during the First General Congregation of the Twelfth Ordinary General Assembly of the Synod of Bishops (October 6, 2008).

29. George Weigel, *Witness to Hope: The Biography of Pope John Paul II* (New York: HarperCollins, 1999), 342.

unity of and continuity between the Old and New Testaments, Scripture and liturgy, faith and reason, and exegesis and dogma. It is a theology that is christological, ecclesiological, and liturgical and culminates in a vision of the kingdom of God in the cosmic liturgy.

As this essay continues, I will explore the foundations and essential principles of Benedict's biblical vision. Next I will consider Benedict's critique of the methods and presumptions of historical and literary criticism of the Bible. I will then consider the key elements of what he calls a "hermeneutic of faith," which restores theology and exegesis to their original ecclesial and liturgical locus. Finally, I will sketch in broad outlines the biblical theology that grows out of Benedict's new hermeneutic before concluding with some reflections on its implications and promise for exegesis and theology.

2

The Critique of Criticism

Beginning the Search
for a New Theological Synthesis

The Historical-Critical Method, an Indispensable Tool

Benedict's theological work shows his deep appropriation of the findings of historical and critical biblical scholarship. In fact, a distinctive feature of his thought is his appreciation for the "historicity" of Christian revelation.[1] The God of Christianity has revealed himself through the mystery of the created world and in historical events in the life of his people, beginning with the patriarch Abraham. Sacred Scripture, reflecting the lived experience of the people of God in the Church, is the vehicle for his revelation in history.

Because God's revelation is inextricably tied to history, Benedict insists that we must study the historical contexts and literary forms in which God's revelation comes to us in order for us to grasp its meaning and appropriate that meaning for ourselves. The methods

1. Aidan Nichols, *The Thought of Benedict XVI: An Introduction to the Theology of Joseph Ratzinger* (London: Burns & Oates, 2005), 292.

of historical study are "important and invaluable" for helping us
understand how biblical texts came to be written and what these
texts might have meant to their original audiences.[2] As he writes
in the methodological prologue to his *Jesus of Nazareth*, "The
historical-critical method—let me repeat—is an indispensable
tool, given the structure of the Christian faith."[3]

His own work, even his homilies and addresses as pope, demonstrates a commanding grasp of New Testament exegesis. He is an
expert on the history of the interpretation of the Gospel of John,
and, in general, his work often presumes knowledge of scholarly
arguments regarding the dating, compositional forms, and original settings of biblical texts. He refers easily and unassumingly
to such things as ancient Near Eastern notions of covenant and
kinship, concepts in Greek philosophy, and definitions in Roman
law. On occasion he has even brought anthropological studies to
bear on his subjects.[4]

Biblical Interpretation in Crisis

Despite his sharp and skillful use of historical-critical methods,
Benedict also has been one of this generation's most forceful critics
of the misuse of these methods. In fact, two of his addresses—
"Biblical Interpretation in Crisis" (1984) and "Faith, Reason, and
the University: Memories and Reflections" (2006)—stand among
the most important statements on higher biblical criticism in the

2. Pope Benedict XVI, Homily, Mass of Possession of the Chair of the Bishop
of Rome (May 7, 2005), in *L'Osservatore Romano*, Weekly Edition in English (May
11, 2005).

3. *Jesus*, xvi. See also *Pierced*, 43–44.

4. See his discussion of the "anthropological basis" of tradition in *Principles*,
86–88. See also *Liturgy*, 117. This natural deployment of the findings of historical and
literary study has become a signature of even his relatively minor catechetical works
as pope. For example, in a homily meditating on the meaning of the priesthood, he
considers not only the use of royal and shepherd imagery in Oriental cultures but also
the use of this imagery in the biblical portraits of Moses and David and the "exilic"
context of Ezekiel's famous prophecy against Israel's shepherds (Ezek. 34). See Pope
Benedict XVI, Homily, Holy Mass for the Ordination to the Priesthood of Fifteen
Deacons of the Diocese of Rome (May 7, 2006), in *L'Osservatore Romano*, Weekly
Edition in English (May 10, 2006), 3.

history of the Church. The methodological prologue of *Jesus of Nazareth* could serve as a summary outline for how to read in a way that moves one "beyond purely historical-critical exegesis so as to apply new methodological insights that allow us to offer a properly theological interpretation of the Bible."[5]

Benedict has called for what amounts to a "critique of criticism." He does not seek to repudiate the methods of modern Scripture study. Instead, he wants to "purify" the historical-critical method through self-examination so it can serve its proper function in the search for the truth of the sacred page. His critique reveals his familiarity with the long history of "scientific" biblical interpretation and with the broader history of ideas since the Reformation.

As Benedict sees it, the "crisis" in modern biblical interpretation is rooted in philosophical, epistemological, and historical assumptions biblical scholars uncritically inherited from the Enlightenment. While they have freely submitted the Bible to all manner of probing and critical analysis, Benedict observes that these scholars have been remarkably unreflective about their own methods and pre-understandings.

> The historico-critical method is essentially a tool, and its usefulness depends on the way in which it is used, that is, on the hermeneutical and philosophical presuppositions one adopts in applying it. In fact there is no such thing as a pure historical method; it is always carried on in a hermeneutical or philosophical context, even when people are not aware of it or expressly deny it. The difficulties which faith continually experiences today in the face of critical exegesis do not stem from the historical or critical factors as such but from the latent philosophy which is at work. The argument, therefore, must relate to this underlying philosophy; it must not attempt to bring historical thought as such under suspicion.[6]

5. *Jesus*, xxiii.
6. *Pierced*, 43. See also his gentle rebuke of the early-twentieth-century Catholic scholar Friedrich Wilhelm Maier: "He did not ask himself to what extent the outlook of the questioner determines access to the text, making it necessary to clarify, above all, the correct way to ask and how best to purify one's own questioning" ("Magisterium").

Its advocates and practitioners claim that the historical-critical method is a true "science" akin to the natural sciences, able to yield findings that are historically accurate and objective. This has been one of the guiding assumptions of modern academic study of the Bible. But in his writing, Benedict frequently invokes the "Heisenberg principle" of uncertainty or indeterminacy. He notes that scientific research has been found to be affected and influenced by researchers' own involvement and presuppositions. "Scientific" biblical criticism, too, has been shaped by scholarly assumptions, which according to Benedict affect everything from the questions scholars pose to the methods they use to the answers and "data" their studies come up with.

Benedict pinpoints several unquestioned yet deep-seated premises that scholars bring to their study of the Bible. The first is a kind of neo-evolutionary model of natural development. This is a premise of the natural sciences that biblical criticism has always seemed anxious to embrace. Evolution posits that later, more-complex life forms evolve from earlier, simpler forms. Applied to Scripture study, this has led exegetes to suppose that "the more theologically considered and sophisticated a text is, the more recent it is, and the simpler something is, the easier it is to reckon it original."[7]

We see this evolutionary hypothesis at work in numerous articles of modern exegetical faith. It appears, for instance, in the obsessive effort to distinguish "Jewish" elements in the Gospels from supposedly later interpolations of "Hellenistic" or Greek philosophy. As Jesus was a Jew with a mission to the Jews, scholars presumed that anything that could not be ascribed to Jewish tradition must be later interpolations from Church leaders influenced by Hellenistic philosophy and culture.[8] We will discuss this aspect more fully below when we take up Benedict's critique of the "de-Hellenization of Christianity." Here it is worth noting, however, that after years of confidently asserting the "Hellenistic" origin of such New Testament details as John's "*Logos*" theology, scholars

7. "Interpretation," 249. See also *Pierced*, 33; *Catechism*, 75.
8. *Pierced*, 33. See also *Catechism*, 75.

now concede that such details in fact reflect deep Jewish and Old Testament themes and concerns, as Benedict points out in *Jesus of Nazareth*.[9] Benedict is never out to score points by identifying discarded scholarly opinions. He wants his readers to see something more fundamental, namely, how the findings of modern exegesis are shaped by exegetes' prior hermeneutical and philosophical positions. His question is this: what grounds justify the modern assumption that religious texts and ideas develop as organisms in nature have been observed to develop? Benedict recognizes evolution as a legitimate theory in the natural sciences[10] but rejects the assumption that religious or spiritual ideas develop along the same evolutionary lines or according to the same evolutionary rules. Such conjecture is hardly self-evident, and, as Benedict points out, there are many contrary examples in the history of Christian spirituality and more generally in the history of ideas.

> First and foremost, one must challenge that basic notion dependent upon a simplistic transferal of science's evolutionary model to spiritual history. Spiritual processes do not follow the rule of zoological genealogies. In fact, it is frequently the opposite. . . . Who would hold that Clement of Rome is more developed or complex than Paul? Is James any more advanced than the Epistle to the Romans? Is the Didache more encompassing than the Pastoral Epistles?[11]

To take one example from Christian spiritual history, we find that the development of *symbol* or the Christian confession of faith reveals an opposite process, one that might be described as *anti*-evolutionary. In trying to articulate its faith in Jesus, the early Church had to choose from a multiplicity of complex names and concepts found in Scripture and in early liturgies and creeds. Jesus was described, among other terms, as prophet, priest, paraclete, angel, Lord, and Son of Man. Through a process of what Bene-

9. *Jesus*, 221, 235.
10. Pope Benedict XVI, Address to the Clergy of the Dioceses of Belluno-Feltre and Treviso (July 24, 2007); but see his cautionary notes on "evolutionism" in *Truth*, 178–82.
11. "Interpretation," 10.

dict calls "increasing simplification and concentration," Church authorities finally settled on the three titles found in the earliest creeds: Christ, Lord, and Son of God.[12]

This historical footnote is intriguing on a number of levels. First, it challenges the assumption that there was some original, primitive simplicity in the way Christians understood the identity of Jesus. It challenges, too, the modern exegetical presumption that creeds and liturgical formulas are later "ecclesial" additions that distorted the meaning of Jesus' original preaching. This brief example not only calls into question the evolutionary hypothesis that underlies modern exegesis but also raises interesting questions about the central role of ecclesial tradition in the formation and redaction of biblical texts. Benedict shows that the earliest Christian witness was decidedly more complex and theologically differentiated than has often been presumed and that it fell to Church authorities to articulate the core or heart of the gospel witness. This is a subject we will return to in the next chapter.

The Correction of Dogma by History

In addition to the neo-evolutionary assumptions of its search for the "primitive element" in Scripture, the historical-critical method also employs an unchallenged and unquestioned hermeneutic of suspicion. Benedict sees this in the general assumption that texts should be studied in isolation from their original ecclesial and liturgical context. In part, this is a logical continuation of biblical scholars' aim to emulate the experimental sciences. To put it perhaps too bluntly, they endeavor to study the biblical texts as a scientist would dissect a specimen in the lab.

To make this point, Benedict returns to the fourth-century debate between the Church Father St. Gregory of Nyssa and the rationalist interlocutor Eunomius. Eunomius believed he could develop an accurate understanding of God by using rational and scientific means exclusively. Gregory disputed this, charging that his opponent's scientific approach "transforms each mystery into a 'thing.'"

12. *Pierced*, 15–17.

Gregory labeled this approach *physiologein*, that is, treating things solely in a "scientific way." Benedict sees this transformation of mysteries into "things" occurring in modern biblical scholarship: "Is there not too much *physiologein* in our exegesis and our modern way of dealing with Scripture? Are we not in fact treating it as we treat matter in the laboratory . . . [as] a dead thing that we assemble and disassemble at our pleasure?"[13]

Benedict's concern raises a basic question concerning method. Why would students of the Bible establish, as a methodological principle, that these religious texts should be studied in isolation from the religious communities that produced these texts and still regard them as sacred and authoritative? The modus operandi of "scientific" exegesis would seem to be wrongheaded for scientific reasons. It would be comparable to a natural scientist deciding to study a plant or animal without any reference to its habitat or its natural environment. Any results gathered using such a method would be, of necessity, partial or incomplete and likely inaccurate.

Benedict suspects that the historical-critical method labors under mistaken assumptions rooted in the Enlightenment's anticlerical wing and perhaps even earlier in the French Encyclopedists' critique of organized religion.[14] He sees this most clearly in the historical-critical study of the Gospels. "Historically speaking," he notes, "this method was first applied at the time of the Enlightenment, with the aim of using history to correct dogma, setting up a purely human, historical Jesus against the Christ of faith."[15]

13. *Song*, 50–51. See also "Interpretation," 254. Gregory's dogmatic treatises *Against Eunomius* and *Answer to Eunomius' Second Book* are translated in *A Select Library of Nicene and Post-Nicene Fathers*, 2nd series, vol. 5, ed. Philip Schaff and Henry Wace (Grand Rapids: Eerdmans, 1994).

14. See the sources assembled in *Principles*, 92n5.

15. *Pierced*, 43. Also *Principles*, 92: "For [Hermann] Reimarus, the Church's faith was no longer the way to find Jesus but a mythical smokescreen that concealed the historical reality. Jesus was to be sought, not *through* dogma, but *against* it, if one wanted to arrive at historical knowledge of him. Historical reason became the corrective of dogma; critical reason became the antipode of traditional faith." See also Joseph Cardinal Ratzinger with Vittorio Messori, *The Ratzinger Report: An Exclusive Interview on the State of the Church*, trans. Salvator Attanasio and Graham Harrison

This more or less anti-ecclesial posture has persisted in exegesis under the influence of such figures as Martin Dibelius and Rudolph Bultmann and their premise of a basic discontinuity between the preaching of Jesus and the post-Easter teachings and traditions of the Church. Even today the scientific exegete presumes that we cannot trust the plain sense of the biblical texts, because the original source traditions have somehow been overlaid with a veneer of Church dogmas and institutional concerns. While seldom stated in such stark terms, that the received biblical texts are a species of ideology—part of the ecclesiastical machinery used to legitimate and consolidate power and control by religious elites—is implicit in the basic operation of biblical "science." In this approach, the Church's traditional use of texts in its dogmas, moral teachings, and liturgical rituals is seen as an impediment, rather than an aid, to understanding the texts' original meanings.

The "Self-Limitation" of Reason

At the root of the historical-critical method is an exaggerated and unnecessary separation between faith and reason. Benedict traces this in part to the epistemological agnosticism or "self-limitation of reason" in the philosophy of the German Enlightenment thinker Immanuel Kant. Kant concluded that it was impossible for human reason to know the truth and reality of "things in themselves," especially God. Historical criticism begins from a similar premise: we can never know for certain about things that transcend our sense perceptions. Hence, the historical method limits itself to studying only the "human element" of the Bible, understood as those things that conform to the evidence of our senses and our understanding of natural laws of causation. This philosophical starting point, Benedict believes, is of "great consequence."

Namely, it is assumed that history is fundamentally and always uniform and that therefore nothing can take place in history but

(San Francisco: Ignatius, 1985), 74–76; Joseph Cardinal Ratzinger, introduction to *The Lord*, by Romano Guardini (Washington, DC: Regnery, 1996 [1954]), xi–xii.

what is possible as a result of causes known to us in nature and in human activity. Aberrations from that, for instance, divine interventions that go beyond the constant interaction of natural and human causes, therefore cannot be historical; the historian must "explain" how such notions could come about. . . . According to this assumption, it is not possible for a man really to be God and to perform deeds that require divine power—actions that would disrupt the general complex of causes. Accordingly, words attributed to Jesus in which he makes divine claims and the corresponding deeds must be "explained." . . . Everything in the figure of Jesus that transcends mere humanity is . . . thus not really historical.[16]

Benedict compares this philosophical turn in biblical exegesis to "the postulate of objectivity" in the natural sciences. This postulate, as formulated by Jacques Monod, the Nobel Prize–winning French biologist, effectively denies that we can know anything about the "causes" or "purposes" of events in the world.[17] Biblical scholarship does essentially the same thing. It denies in principle that we can know with certainty anything about whether God acts or causes anything to happen in the world. Of the events in the Bible, we can know only what we are capable of knowing through the operations of reason and science. Put simply, from what we see in ordinary life and from what we know about natural laws of causation, we do not know of men being able to walk on water, multiply loaves of bread and fishes, or rise from the dead. As a result, the biblical exegete can tell us nothing about biblical texts that speak of such activities.

Practically speaking, then, this prior philosophical assumption makes it impossible for the exegete to reckon with much of the New Testament, not to mention the rest of the Bible. The exegete must bracket off as pious exaggerations or legends every claim made in the texts about miracles or God's work in the world and in history. This puts historical critics in the position of having

16. *Way*, 61–62. See also "Interpretation," 254: "Modern exegesis . . . completely relegated God to the incomprehensible in order to be able to treat the biblical text as an entirely worldly reality according to natural-scientific methods."

17. See Benedict's discussion of Monod in *Way*, 63–65.

to explain away rather than to explicate the plain sense of many
biblical texts.[18]

The Limits of the Historical-Critical Method

These unquestioned assumptions of the historical-critical method—
its neo-evolutionary impulse, its isolation of the biblical text from
the Church, and its rigid separation of reason and faith—have
sharply limited this method's usefulness. Indeed, the power of
Benedict's critique lies in its insistence that we evaluate the merits
of the method purely on "scientific" grounds. Does the method
"work," that is, does it have the power to explain things? Benedict
believes that because of its prior assumptions, the method doesn't
explain as much as it could or should.

> The historico-critical method is a marvelous instrument for read-
> ing historical sources and interpreting texts. But it does include
> its own philosophy, which generally—if, for instance, I want to
> learn about the medieval emperors—hardly affects anything.
> For in that case I want to learn about the past, that is all. . . . If
> you apply it to the Bible, then two factors you would otherwise
> scarcely notice are clearly manifest: the method seeks to know
> about the past as something past. It seeks to know what hap-
> pened then, in the form it took then, at the point at which things
> stood right then.
>
> And it assumes that all history is in principle the same kind of
> history: man in all his different manifestations, the world in all
> its manifold variety, are yet determined by the same laws and the
> same limitations, so that I can eliminate what is impossible. What
> cannot possibly happen could not have happened yesterday and,
> likewise, cannot be going to happen tomorrow. If we apply this
> to the Bible, it means that a text, an event, or a person is strictly
> fixed in his or its place in the past. We are seeking to bring out
> what the writer said at the time and what he could have said or
> thought at the time. It is a matter of what is "historical," what
> was "current at the time."

18. *Song*, 30.

That is why historico-critical exegesis does not transmit the
Bible to today, into my present-day life. The possibility has been
excluded. On the contrary, it distances it from me and shows it as
firmly set in the past. . . . Of its nature, it does not speak about today,
or about me, but about yesterday, about other people. Therefore it
can never show Christ yesterday, today, and forever, but only (if it
remains true to itself) Christ as he was yesterday.[19]

This, for Benedict, is the most obvious limitation of the historical-
critical method—of its nature it can only yield hypotheses about
the past, about what might have been the case.[20]

The overarching error of the historical-critical method, as he
sees it, is the removal of the Bible from its natural "habitat" in the
Church. The faith of the Church is what gives the Bible its continued relevance, its unity, and its quality as revelatory speech. The
method can certainly help us understand the contexts of events and
ideas found in the Scriptures and what the words might have meant
to their original audiences. But without reference to the meaning
these texts possess in the Church's life and liturgy, the Scriptures
become a kind of dead letter, an artifact from a long-extinct exotic
culture. Biblical exegesis becomes an exercise in "antiquarianism"
or "archaeology" or perhaps "necrophilia."[21]

Another consequence of the separation of the Bible from
the Church is a loss of any unified perspective. The Church makes
the various individual texts into a single book or "Bible." Without the Church we have only a jumble of unconnected texts. As a
result, the study of the scriptural texts moves away from the actual words on the page to the formulation of various unprovable
hypotheses about questions related to the production of the text:
who wrote it, who it was originally intended for, what were the
various stages in the writing and editing of the text. As Benedict
says: "The dismemberment of the Bible has led to a new variety
of allegorism. One no longer reads the text but the supposed ex-

19. *Truth*, 132–33.
20. See *Jesus*, xvi.
21. *Theology*, 65, 95. "We cannot reach Christ through historical reconstruction.
It may be helpful, but it is not sufficient and, on its own, becomes necrophilia" (*Faith*,
28). See also *Jesus*, xvi.

perience of supposed communities. The result is an often highly
fanciful allegorical interpretation, which turns out to be a means
of self-affirmation for the interpreter."[22] In other words, the drift
of the method is away from reading the Bible as it is given to us
and toward hypothetical reconstructions of the Bible, in which the
meaning of the texts often resembles what the interpreter thinks
the text ought to have said.

Finally, Benedict faults the method's rigid refusal to consider a
supernatural or divine object in the biblical texts, a refusal based
on a self-limitation of reason and a view of "the homogeneity of
all history, according to which nothing can really have happened
except what could always happen."[23] This, as we have seen, leads
the exegete to remain silent in the face of such biblical phenomena
as Christ's resurrection from the dead.

Moreover, it results in a curious "subjectivizing" of Scripture.
Since the words of Scripture presumably are unable to give us true
"objective" information about God, Jesus, or transcendent realities,
"everything having to do with God and his appearance in history
must be relegated to the experience and feelings of the subject."
This means, for instance, that the New Testament witness to Jesus'
relationship with the Father must be explained simply by means of
Jesus' "special experience of God," not his identity as God.[24]

The De-Hellenization of Christianity

For Benedict, then, it becomes essential that we "recognize the
limits of the historical-critical method"[25] and "purify" the method
by removing those assumptions and prior understandings that
limit its usefulness. This purification requires a thoroughgoing
reevaluation of the modern relationship between faith and reason.
This has become an increasingly urgent theme in the writings and
talks of the pope. It was the subject of one of the most important

22. *Theology*, 65.
23. Joseph Cardinal Ratzinger, "An Event That Preceded Their Thinking and
Willing," *30 Days* (May 2004).
24. *Way*, 64.
25. *Jesus*, xvi.

programmatic addresses of his pontificate, "Faith, Reason, and the University," delivered at Regensburg University in 2006.

In this address, Benedict situates the crisis in biblical interpretation within the context of a wider, more disturbing breakdown of the synthesis of faith and reason worked out at the beginning of Christianity. He sees this breakdown as the outcome of a long, historical effort aimed at the "de-Hellenization of Christianity."[26]

This process began in the Middle Ages and reached its full flower in the Reformation with Martin Luther's efforts to remove the influences of Catholic philosophy and dogma and return to what he believed to be the original purity of Scripture alone. In different forms, the *sola Scriptura* principle became a key premise of the liberal theology of the nineteenth and twentieth centuries. In seeking the unadulterated message and person of Jesus, liberal theology treated the biblical Word as a historical record to be read without reference to philosophical and theological formulations made using Greek language and Greek philosophical tools. This meant returning to a kind of literalism uninformed by such products of philosophical reasoning as the doctrines concerning the Trinity and the divinity of Christ.

This new theological outlook was greatly influenced by the rise of the natural sciences and the achievements of technology, as well as by Kant's philosophical "self-limitation of reason" to only those things that can be perceived by the senses. These influences, in turn, gave rise to the modern understanding that truth and certainty are a function of what can be observed and either verified or falsified through experimentation in the laboratory.

Human reason in the modern period has since come to be seen as limited strictly to seeking understandings that conform to these "scientific" canons of truth and certainty. Because they cannot be answered according to these modern canons, questions about such things as the existence of God or the meaning of human existence are discarded as "unscientific or prescientific." Hence, religious faith in the modern age is no longer viewed as a source of true

26. Pope Benedict XVI, "Faith, Reason, and the University: Memories and Reflections," Lecture at Aula Magna of the University of Regensburg (September 12, 2006).

knowledge about humans and the world; rather, it is regarded as a feeling or sentiment and a matter of individual or subjective preference.

According to Benedict, these developments—the separation of faith and reason and the radical diminution of both these faculties of the human spirit—are the root cause of grave problems in the world today. The entire project of de-Hellenization, as he sees it, rests on a false premise, namely, that the Christian faith can or should be separated from human reason as it was understood in the Hellenistic world. This premise is false because, as Benedict argues, "the encounter between the biblical message and Greek thought did not happen by chance." He cites St. Paul's vision of a Greek man calling Paul to "come over to Macedonia and help us" (Acts 16:6–10). Benedict interprets this vision as indicating "the intrinsic necessity of a rapprochement between Biblical faith and Greek inquiry."[27]

He notes that the Gospels themselves were written in the Greek language, using vocabulary and concepts drawn from the Hellenistic milieu. The same influences can be found in the Jewish people—who lived for many decades under Hellenistic rule. Notwithstanding their oppression, they too "encountered the best of Greek thought at a deep level." The fruits of that encounter can be seen within the Scriptures themselves in the so-called wisdom literature. An even more compelling testimony of Greek influence is the translation known as the Septuagint, which Benedict describes as "more than a simple (and in that sense really less than satisfactory) translation of the Hebrew text: it is an independent textual witness and a distinct and important step in the history of revelation, one which brought about this encounter in a way that was decisive for the birth and spread of Christianity."[28]

For Benedict, all this means that "the fundamental decisions made about the relationship between faith and the use of human reason are part of the faith itself; they are developments consonant

27. Benedict XVI, "Faith, Reason, and the University."
28. Benedict XVI, "Faith, Reason, and the University."

with the nature of faith itself."[29] Moreover, he says, there is no need for us to think of human reason in such restricted terms as limited to seeking to understand only phenomena that can be seen or experienced. The self-limitation of reason has given rise to "the dictatorship of appearances." It has become "a kind of dogma" that we cannot know anything more than what is apparent.[30]

But Benedict stresses the correspondence between what reason has enabled us to discover about the natural world and the truths revealed by biblical faith. Modern science and technology are based on fundamental observations about the "rationality" of the natural world, that matter is structured in an orderly mathematic and rational way and that it operates according to predictable laws that can be detected and manipulated by human reason. These observations about the natural world are remarkably consistent with biblical faith in God, who is the creative *Logos* or Reason.[31]

Benedict reminds us that the biblical witness describes a God who is reasonable and who gives us reason as one means by which we can know him:

> Here we can see the profound harmony between what is Greek in the best sense of the word and the biblical understanding of faith in God. Modifying the first verse of the Book of Genesis, the first verse of the whole Bible, John began the prologue of his Gospel with the words: "In the beginning was the *Logos*." . . . *Logos* means both reason and word—a reason which is creative and capable of self-communication, precisely as reason. John thus spoke the final word on the biblical concept of God, and in this word all the often toilsome and tortuous threads of biblical faith find their culmination and synthesis. In the beginning was the *logos*, and the *logos* is God, says the Evangelist.[32]

29. Benedict XVI, "Faith, Reason, and the University." See also Address to the Youth of Rome and the Lazio Region in Preparation for World Youth Day (April 6, 2006); Address to Participants of the Fourth National Ecclesial Convention of Verona (October 19, 2006).

30. Joseph Cardinal Ratzinger, "Culture and Truth: Some Reflections on the Encyclical Letter *Fides et Ratio*" (1999), in *Benedict XVI*, 375.

31. *Truth*, 156–58.

32. Benedict XVI, "Faith, Reason, and the University."

Thus Benedict believes that human reason, through its study of the world and its invention of theories and technologies, naturally points beyond itself, beyond the world of appearances and sense phenomena, to God: "The concept of reason needs instead to be 'broadened' in order to be able to explore and embrace those aspects of reality which go beyond the purely empirical."[33]

As we will see, Benedict's own approach to exegesis and biblical theology is itself the fruit of his belief in the profound harmony of faith and reason in the search for God's plan for the world and the truth of revelation.

33. Pope Benedict XVI, Address to the Participants in the First European Meeting of University Lecturers (June 23, 2007).

3

The Hermeneutic of Faith

Critical and Historical Foundations for a Biblical Theology

The Legitimacy of Interpretation

We have seen that Benedict takes historical criticism's "scientific" intentions seriously. His critique of criticism is built solidly on scientific and methodological grounds. In one of his most important statements on theological and exegetical method, he writes:

> From a purely scientific point of view, the legitimacy of an interpretation depends on its power to explain things. In other words, the less it needs to interfere with the sources, the more it respects the corpus as given and is able to show it to be intelligible from within, by its own logic, the more apposite such an interpretation is. Conversely, the more it interferes with the sources, the more it feels obliged to excise and throw doubt on things found there, the more alien to the subject it is. To that extent, its explanatory power is also its ability to maintain the inner unity of the corpus in question. It involves the ability to unify, to achieve a synthesis, which is the reverse of superficial harmonization. Indeed, only faith's hermeneutic is sufficient to measure up to these criteria.[1]

1. *Pierced*, 44–45.

Before we look in detail at Benedict's "hermeneutic of faith," we need to look once more in a summary fashion at the methodological problems of historical criticism. At a basic level, the problem is obvious. Historical criticism is a method for studying religious texts that is unable to adequately explain the religious meaning of these texts. From the standpoint of science, that is, in terms of its "power to explain things," the method is found wanting. Its hermeneutic of suspicion vis-à-vis the faith of the Church, the presumption of neo-evolutionary patterns of development in the texts, and the excising of reference to supernatural phenomena require a high degree of interference with the biblical sources as they have been given to us. Nor does the method exhibit any capacity to preserve or identify an inner unity or inner logic within the texts. As a result, Benedict says, modern exegesis can never provide more than conjectures and hypotheses, all of which are constantly subject to being contradicted and replaced by later theories.

> By its very nature, historical interpretation can never take us beyond hypotheses. After all, none of us was there when it happened; only physical science can repeat events in the laboratory.[2]

> It is becoming apparent that any interpretation that is detached from the life of the Church and from her historical experiences remains non-obligatory and cannot rise above the literary genre of a hypothesis, which has to reckon with the possibility of being rendered obsolete at any time, just like any other ephemeral saying.[3]

But there are even more serious consequences at the intersection of biblical interpretation and Christian faith. Benedict warned the bishops of the world gathered for the synod on sacred Scripture that at stake is nothing less than the belief in the resurrection, the core of Christian faith:

> The first consequence . . . is that the Bible becomes solely a history book. Moral consequences can be drawn from it, history can be

2. *Catechism*, 67–68.
3. *Way*, 152.

learned from it, but the book as such speaks of history alone and exegesis is no longer truly theological but instead becomes purely historiographical, literary history. This is the first consequence: the Bible remains in the past, speaks only of the past.

The second consequence is even graver: where the hermeneutics of faith . . . disappear, another type of hermeneutics will appear by necessity—a hermeneutics that is secularist, positivist, the key fundamental of which is the conviction that the divine does not appear in human history. According to this hermeneutics, when there seems to be a divine element, the source of that impression must be explained, thus reducing everything to the human element. As a result, it is the grounds for interpretations that deny the historicity of divine elements.

Today the exegetical "mainstream" in Germany, for example, denies that the Lord instituted the Holy Eucharist and says that Jesus' corpse remained in the tomb. . . . This happens because the hermeneutics of faith is missing: profane philosophical hermeneutics is affirmed instead, which deny the possibility of the entrance and presence of the divine in history. . . .

When exegesis is not theological, Scripture cannot be the soul of theology, and vice versa; when theology is not essentially Scriptural interpretation within the Church, then this theology no longer has a foundation. Therefore, for the life and mission of the Church, for the future of faith, it is absolutely necessary to overcome this dualism between exegesis and theology. Biblical theology and systematic theology are two dimensions of one reality, which we call theology.[4]

This is as compact and profound a statement as one might wish of Benedict's project—both as a pastor and as a scholar. Indeed, Benedict has defined his pontificate in these terms: "Leading men and women to God, to the God who speaks in the Bible: this is the supreme and fundamental priority of the Church and of the successor of Peter at the present time."[5] He insists that for the fu-

4. Pope Benedict XVI, Address during the Fourteenth General Congregation of the Twelfth Ordinary General Assembly of the Synod of Bishops (October 14, 2008).
5. Pope Benedict XVI, Letter to the Bishops of the Catholic Church concerning the Remission of the Excommunication of the Four Bishops Consecrated by Archbishop Lefebvre (March 10, 2009).

ture of the faith itself we must overcome the dualism that divides exegesis and theology; we must once more make Scripture the soul of a theology that is simultaneously biblical and systematic.

For Benedict, literary and historical study of the Scriptures will always remain an "absolute necessity."[6] That is because divine revelation is historical. Indeed, both Judaism and Christianity are religions of history. The texts of Scripture not only include legal, ethical, and liturgical prescriptions or inspirational legends but also are essentially historical works, chronicling God's interventions in human history and his ongoing relationship with his chosen people, the people of God. Hence it is essential to study the historical and literary contexts of the texts of the Bible in order to appreciate their rich depths and manifold meanings.

Historical and literary methods alone, however, are not sufficient. This is because historical study, as we have seen, can give us only hypotheses of varying degrees of certitude. Further, the biblical texts are more than ancient documents written in human words, because these words point beyond themselves. They are also the living and revealed Word of God addressed to men and women of faith at that particular moment in history and at this moment in time. Reason and the methods of historical and literary science must therefore be joined to the living faith of the Church to which God's Word is always being addressed. Bringing the truths of faith to bear on biblical questions does not stifle reason but rather frees it from the prisons of its own self-imposed limitations. The cooperation of faith and reason holds open the promise of understanding the true meaning of the events and teachings found in Scripture.

> It should . . . be borne in mind that the true meaning of historical facts—even in profane matters—is not revealed by a mere photo-graphical recording of facts as such, but unfolds only in a light that comes from elsewhere, from a vision of reality which can never be simply reduced to the limited horizons of a fact empirically considered. From this point of view, it is even logical that the interpretation of faith cannot be indisputably imposed on the historian. What

6. "Magisterium." See also *Jesus*, xv.

is essential, however, is that such an interpretation should not be excluded from the facts.[7]

We see in this passage Benedict's gentle insistence: the Scriptures are not to be read by "faith alone," but we cannot exclude the insights of faith, as so much of modern exegesis does.

The Explanatory Power of Faith's Hermeneutic

The "hermeneutic of faith"[8] proposed by Benedict is less an interpretive "system" than it is a spiritual disposition toward the study of the sacred page. As we will see in the chapters that follow, it is perhaps best described as a kind of loving and reverent listening, a seeking after the living voice of God who in his gracious love speaks to man in the human words of the biblical texts. To assist with this listening, Benedict employs the critical tools of modern exegetical science along with ancient interpretive methods and perspectives drawn from the Church's dogmatic, liturgical, and homiletic traditions.

In his exegetical and theological writing, we see the superior explanatory power of this hermeneutic of faith, which rejects artificial delimitations imposed on reason and insists that faith is a legitimate source of knowledge. Benedict argues that in addition to the essential scientific study, faith is necessary for a full understanding of the texts, which in their most literal sense speak of experiences and realities that transcend human experience. In the following passage, we again see Benedict's appreciation of the profound unity of faith and reason and glimpse his broader critique of modern rationalism.

> Faith has a contribution to make with regard to the interpretation of Scripture. . . . To reduce all of reality as we meet it to pure material causes, to confine the Creator Spirit to the sphere of mere subjectivity, is irreconcilable with the fundamental message of the

---

7. Joseph Cardinal Ratzinger, "Question of Truth Lies at Center of Theology," *L'Osservatore Romano*, Weekly Edition in English (January 1, 1997).
   8. *Eschatology*, 272.

Bible. This involves, however, a debate on the very nature of true rationality; since, if a purely materialistic explanation of reality is presented as the only possible expression of reason, then reason itself is falsely understood. . . .

Faith itself is a way of knowing. Wanting to set it aside does not produce pure objectivity, but comprises a point of view which excludes a particular perspective while not wanting to take into account the accompanying conditions of the chosen point of view. If one takes into account, however, that the sacred Scriptures come from God through a subject which lives continually—the pilgrim people of God—then it becomes clear rationally as well that this subject has something to say about the understanding of the book.[9]

In this passage we see the fundamental elements of Benedict's approach to the Bible. Reading Scripture is a dialogue in faith with the God who speaks to us from the living experience of his people, the Church. The Scriptures cannot be read apart from the Church, for the Church is the subject that God's Word continually addresses. And the Scriptures cannot be understood without taking into account the faith that the Word of God seeks from its readers.

Apostolic Succession, the Canon, and the Rule of Faith

As we have said, Benedict does not propose a theological system, let alone a philosophy of interpretation. His hermeneutic of faith arises organically from the historical structure of revelation itself, that is, from the historical processes whereby the Scriptures were written down and handed on in the Church. The recognition of this structure of revelation is one of the important findings of modern form and redaction criticism. By studying the complex processes by which the Scriptures originated and were shaped over long years by the Church's preaching, teaching, and worship, scholars have discovered what Benedict describes as an "interwoven relationship between Church and Bible, between the people of God and the Word of God."[10]

9. "Magisterium"; emphasis added.
10. *Pilgrim*, 32–33.

Unfortunately, historical and literary scholarship generally has not pursued the methodological implications of its own conclusions. The methods of historical criticism are primarily based on modern scientific and philosophic principles that are then applied to—some might say imposed on—the biblical texts. Benedict starts in a different place, a place suggested by what we know historically about how the Scriptures were composed, edited, and transmitted. His hermeneutic of faith begins in the heart of the Church, where the task of understanding and interpreting Scripture is part of the Church's larger response to the divine Word that has been spoken to it. For this reason, Benedict's hermeneutic embraces elements of the Church's response to the Word that are explicitly rejected by historical critics—for instance, the Church's doctrinal, sacramental, and liturgical traditions as well as the traditions of "spiritual" interpretation found in the earliest Christian teachings.

To appreciate the forcefulness of Benedict's hermeneutic and his theological project, we need to consider his historical recovery of early Christianity. This recovery demonstrates the inseparable bond, the original unity of Word, sacrament, Church authority, and tradition. In studying this retrieval, we will be able to see how Benedict locates in the very foundations of the Church the grounds for his own principle presuppositions about the reading of sacred Scripture.

He focuses on three critical "establishments" in the early Church. First, the establishment of *apostolic succession*, the tradition of Church government and ministry that guarantees the faithful transmission of the apostles' witness and teaching to future generations. Second, the establishment of the *canon*, the list of those texts deemed by Church authorities to be truly the Word of God. And finally, the "rule of faith" (*regula fidei*), established to guarantee the Church's authentic interpretation of the Word of God consistent with the witness of the apostles.

These "establishments" illuminate the historical continuity between the Church of Jesus Christ and Israel, who are the people of God, and hence between the gospel of Christ and the Word spoken by God to Israel, that is, the Word of the Law and the covenant. As we go deeper into Benedict's biblical worldview, we will have occasion to explore the breadth of his vision of Israel and the Church. Here we will hit a few of the high notes: Benedict sees the essential continuity of Israel and the Church in the Christian affirmation that Jesus is the long-expected Messiah of Israel, in Jesus' preaching that his gospel is the fulfillment of Israel's Torah, and in the Eucharist as the fulfillment of Israel's Passover.

The apostolic structure of the Church, too, is an essential mark of continuity with Israel; the twelve chosen by Jesus deliberately evokes the twelve tribes of Israel.[11] Establishment of the canon acknowledged the "sovereignty of the Word" and the Church as servant of the Word. At the same time it fixed the form of that Word, establishing the New Testament and the Hebrew Scriptures as "a single Scripture" and "master text." The Word and the Church's witness to that Word cannot be separated. Thus the continuity of that witness through history is guaranteed by the establishment of apostolic succession and the episcopal ministry. Finally, the truth of that witness is guaranteed by the rule of faith, which becomes "a key for interpretation."

These historical establishments testify to a "reciprocal compenetration" among the Word of God, the Church's apostolic witness to that Word, and the Church's rule of faith.[12] Benedict goes so far as to state boldly: "The establishment of the canon and the establishment of the early Church are one and the same process but viewed from different perspectives."[13]

In Benedict's vision, the Church is a communion with the living God in the body of Christ effected by the Word and by the faithful response to the Word in the sacraments. The Church is united by the Word, built up by the Word, and given a mission to serve the Word. The sweeping "Word-centeredness" of

11. *Communion*, 25. Pope Benedict XVI, "Christ and the Church," General Audience (March 15, 2006).

12. Pope Benedict XVI, Address to Ecumenical Meeting at the Archbishopric of Cologne (August 19, 2005), in *L'Osservatore Romano*, Weekly Edition in English (August 24, 2005), 8–9.

13. *Principles*, 148.

Benedict's ecclesiology is truly remarkable and unparalleled among theologians of his generation, Catholic or otherwise. He understands all the essential constituent elements of the Church—the hierarchy of apostolic succession, the apostolic tradition, the canon of Scripture, the Creed, and the rule of faith—in relation to the revelation and mission of the Word of God. For instance, apostolic succession is not merely a mechanism for filling vacant Church leadership offices. It is rather, for Benedict, "a dedication to the Word, an office bearing witness to the treasure with which one has been entrusted." He adds: "The office, the apostolic succession, is grounded in the Word. . . . In fact, succession equals Tradition. Succession means cleaving to the apostolic Word, just as Tradition means the continuance of authorized witnesses."[14]

In this cleaving to the Word, the successors to the apostles make the divine Word concrete in our day, thereby making the Church "the living presence of the divine Word."[15] Here again we see that Benedict's understanding of the relationship of Word and Church tends toward the sacramental, even the mystical. The Church is called into being by the Word and lives by the power of the Word. At the same time, God entrusts his Word and its interpretation to the Church, commissioning the Church to draw all men and women into communion through their hearing and believing in the Word.

For Benedict, the office of the apostle is a sharing in the divine power of Christ. He finds support for this in Christ commissioning the apostles: "Anyone who listens to you listens to me; anyone who rejects you rejects me" and again, "As the Father sent me, so I am sending you." The apostle is more than a spokesman for Christ, however. He proclaims the same words as Christ, announcing the coming of the kingdom of God. But he also, by the divine gift, "has the power to make the coming visible by signs of power."[16]

14. "Primacy," 47–48.
15. "Primacy," 59.
16. *Principles*, 273–74. See Luke 10:16; Matt. 10:7–9, 40; John 20:21; Mark 3:14–19, respectively.

The principle of apostolic succession becomes the hinge of Benedict's ecclesiology. The Church is the bearer of the tradition of Christ and the subject that the Word addresses down through history. The teaching of the apostles becomes the source of "their abiding presence in the Church," uniting future generations with the Word entrusted to the first apostles.[17] But the apostolic Word abides in power through the priestly ministry established by the apostles. The priestly ministry, we will see, is central to Benedict's understanding of the Church and its role in salvation history.[18] Here we want to note only that the priestly ministry is an expression of the apostolic witness that is foundational to the Church in Benedict's historical reconstruction. Through the priestly ministry, the revealed Word becomes sacrament, bringing forth the kingdom proclaimed by Christ and bringing the world into communion with the divine.

The Tradition: Church as *Memoria Ecclesiae, Viva Vox*

The Church is the living voice, the *viva vox*,[19] of the Word of God. As the living, historical subject addressed by the divine Word[20] that also bears witness to its encounter with the Word in history, the Church serves as a sort of collective memory for humankind, providing a unifying narrative for human history. Benedict speaks of "the *memoria Ecclesiae*, the memory of the Church, the Church as memory."[21] As the living voice of the Word, the Church bears the memory of God's saving acts in history, most decisively the event of Christ's descent from heaven and entrance into history.

Here we enter into Benedict's distinctive treatment of the nature of sacred tradition and its relation to sacred Scripture. Benedict builds on the Second Vatican Council's teaching on tradition,[22] presuming a broad understanding of divine revelation as the sum

17. *Pilgrim*, 64.
18. *Communion*, 111–25.
19. *Pilgrim*, 35.
20. *Liturgy*, 167–69; *Theology*, 94.
21. *Principles*, 23.
22. See *Dei Verbum* 7–10.

of the ways in which God in his merciful condescension makes himself known to men and women in history. In this understanding, the written Scriptures form just one part, however important, of God's effort to communicate himself and his will to us.

It is true, as "scientific exegesis" has demonstrated, that "the Gospels are a product of the early Church—indeed . . . the whole of Scripture is nothing other than Tradition."[23] But for Benedict, the sacred tradition of the Church cannot be reduced to a treasure chest, a static collection of ancient texts, legislations, and venerable practices. Scripture is at the center of the Church's tradition,[24] but tradition is properly understood as the whole of "the responsive Word of the Church"[25]—a living dialogue in which the Church constantly listens to the Word addressed to her and responds to the claims the Word makes on her through her preaching, teaching, doctrine, and liturgy.

More than that, tradition is a participation in the power of God promised to the Church by Christ. It is nothing other than the fulfillment of Christ's promise to be with his Church in the Spirit until the end of the age (Matt. 28:20). As Benedict describes it, tradition is the "permanent actualization of the active presence of the Lord Jesus in his People, brought about by the Holy Spirit and expressed in the Church through the apostolic ministry and fraternal communion."[26]

Tradition, then, is nothing less than Christ's living and saving and *interpretive* presence in the Church. Benedict reminds us that in the early Church the Word of God did not primarily refer to a book. The writers of the New Testament considered the "Scriptures" to be the Jewish Scriptures, what we today call the "Old Testament." In the argument of Paul, the old covenant writings were the *gramma* ("letter") while the preaching of the new covenant was the *pneuma* ("spirit"). Indeed, the preaching that led to the writings of the New

23. Joseph Cardinal Ratzinger with Vittorio Messori, *The Ratzinger Report: An Exclusive Interview on the State of the Church*, trans. Salvator Attanasio and Graham Harrison (San Francisco: Ignatius, 1985), 160.

24. "Magisterium."

25. *Liturgy*, 169.

26. "Primacy," 49–53.

Testament was considered to be the Spirit of Christ, or "the Christ-event as the Spirit which explains Scripture."[27]

Here we see Benedict's full meaning in identifying Scripture with tradition. Behind all the tradition is the gift of the revelation of Christ. "Tradition by its very nature is always interpretation."[28] It is the authoritative and enduring presence of the Spirit of Christ in his Church, which interprets the Old Testament "on the basis of the Christ-event and as oriented to that event." In other words, the Church interprets the Christ-event as the fulfillment of the Old Testament.[29]

The presence of Christ is inseparable from the authority of the Church, which ensures that what we do today as believers in Christ is authentically and authoritatively connected to the experience and witness of the apostles. To explain this, Benedict draws on biblical imagery of the Church as the temple of God and the sacraments as the living blood and water flowing from Christ.

> Tradition is the practical continuity of the Church, the holy Temple of God the Father, built on the foundation of the apostles and held together by the cornerstone, Christ, through the life-giving action of the Spirit. . . . Thanks to Tradition, guaranteed by the ministry of the apostles and by their successors, the water of life that flowed from Christ's side and his saving blood reach the women and men of all times. . . . Tradition is not the transmission of things or words, a collection of dead things. Tradition is the living river that links us to the origins, the living river in which the origins are ever present, the great river that leads us to the gates of eternity.[30]

We see again Benedict's insistence on the "interwovenness" of the Church and the tradition. The "temple" of Christ's body spoken of in the Gospels becomes the Church, the life-blood of which becomes the sacred tradition that includes not only the Word that

27. See 2 Cor. 3:6–18. See also the discussion in "Revelation," 37–39 and "Primacy," 49–53.

28. "Revelation," 46.

29. "Revelation," 41–42.

30. Pope Benedict XVI, General Audience (April 26, 2006), in *L'Osservatore Romano*, Weekly Edition in English (May 3, 2006), 11. Cf. John 7:38; 19:34; Eph. 2:19–22; Rev. 21:6, 9–14; 22:1, 17.

the Church speaks but also the principle of succession by which it guarantees both its authentic union with Christ and the Church's life-giving power to bring people to the gates of heaven. All of this is rooted in the promise of Christ to his apostles. In the tradition of the Church, Christ remains with the Church and "through the Spirit, expounds to the disciples what they once were unable to bear, when the Lord still visibly dwelt among them (John 16:12)."[31]

The Primacy of the Liturgical and Sacramental

What is unmistakable in Benedict's recovery of Christian origins is the essential unity of the Church and the Word. And everything in the Church, all the instruments of tradition—the canon of Scripture, the *regula fidei*, the teachings of the Church, its dogmas and creeds, and all the rest—are ordered to the Church's mission, which is to spread the Word of God and to make all men and women believers in the Word. The Word is always the Word that is *heard*, a word that summons the hearer to communion with the living Voice that speaks. That communion is consummated in the affirmation of the Word in the Creed and in the sacraments of baptism and the Eucharist. The Word, then, cannot be separated from the Church's doctrinal and liturgical tradition.

Historically speaking, from the beginning the Word was inseparable from the Church's liturgy and its creedal formulations. Benedict notes that from the start the criteria for determining which texts to include in the canon were liturgical and sacramental in nature. "A book was recognized as 'canonical' if it was sanctioned by the Church for use in public worship. . . . In the ancient Church, the reading of Scripture and the confession of faith were primarily liturgical acts of the whole assembly gathered around the risen Lord."[32]

The Church's sacramental liturgy, then, both shaped the canon and was the original form of the Church's confession of faith. This once more points to the interwoven relationship of the threefold establishment of apostolic succession, canon, and the rule of faith.

31. "Revelation," 39.
32. *Principles*, 148; see also 150.

The original sphere of existence of the Christian profession of faith
. . . was the sacramental life of the Church. It is by this criterion
that the canon was shaped, and that is why the Creed is the primary authority for the interpretation of the Bible. Yet the Creed is
not a piece of literature: for a long time, people quite consciously
avoided writing down the rule of faith that produced the Creed,
just because it is the concrete life of the believing community. Thus,
the authority of the Church that speaks out, the authority of the
apostolic succession, is written into Scripture through the Creed
and is indivisible from it. The teaching office of the apostles' successors does not represent a second authority alongside Scripture
but is inwardly part of it.[33]

We begin to see here another identifying feature of Benedict's
historical understanding of the Church: his accent on the centrality
of liturgy. This too will become important when we begin to consider
his biblical theology. The Word in the Church is always a summons to
worship and adoration, to the encounter with Christ in the Eucharist.
The description of the early Church in Acts 2:42 ("They devoted
themselves to the apostles' teaching and fellowship [*koinonia*], to
the breaking of bread and the prayers") is decisive for him:

> We can see in this a sketch of the primitive Christian service of wor-
> ship, which starts with the teaching of the apostles, that is, with the
> proclamation and hearing of the faith of the Church, of the Word of
> God that is alive in her and that thus becomes the basis for liturgical
> and living fellowship: it reaches a climax in the eucharistic encounter
> with the Lord, who gives himself to us as bread, and resounds in
> songs of praise. The Church is adoration. This passage is telling us
> that the Church subsists as liturgy and in liturgy.[34]

"A Word about the Word": The Structure of Christian Faith

In Benedict's historical retrieval of the original structure of revelation and the Church, the Word of God summons the Church into
being and presses the Church into service. The Word is entrusted

33. *Pilgrim*, 35.
34. *Eucharist*, 121–22. See also *Pilgrim*, 63–65.

to the Church by Christ, who commands the Church to proclaim it to the ends of the earth. The Word proclaimed is always a Word that seeks conversion. As such, the Word always leads to the sacraments, to the enactment or "actualization" of the Word by which the believer enters into communion with the Word, sharing in the life of God and being made a part of the family of God.

This movement of Word to sacramental actualization is also a part of the original structure of revelation and the Church, according to Benedict. The Word made flesh, Jesus Christ, comes to call a people together into a "kingdom," which is a covenant relationship with God. This covenant is made in Christ's death and resurrection and, by his command, is to be remembered and renewed in the sacramental-liturgical action of the Eucharist. So Benedict can say: "The Church is . . . the communion of the Word and Body of Christ and is thus communion among men. . . . The Church is effectively realized in the eucharistic celebration, in which the Word of preaching likewise becomes present."[35]

The Church's mission is to extend that communion with God to the ends of the earth—through the preaching of the Word and the making present of that Word in the sacraments. In this mission, the Church must be considered a sacrament, for it is the historical actualization of the Word of God as the people of God. The Church and all of its sacraments are indeed communications of Christ, "communications of him who, because he is God's visible Word, is truly the founder of the Christian sacrament."[36]

In the Church's preaching and liturgy, the "seeming past word and action of Jesus" become "a present reality." By the Word, actualized in the sacraments, believers have "contemporaneity with Christ."[37] Historically speaking, then, the Church's identity has been defined from the beginning by these two pillars: Word and sacrament.[38] This original self-understanding of the Church stems from the mandates given by Christ himself, both at the Last Supper

35. *Communion*, 76–77.
36. *Principles*, 47.
37. *Theology*, 60. See also *Principles*, 88, 100.
38. See "Primacy," 45: "Sacrament *and* Word are the two pillars on which the Church stands."

("Do this in memory of me") and on the mount in Galilee ("Go therefore and make disciples of all nations, baptizing them . . ."). As Benedict points out: "The universalism of salvation . . . requires that the Easter memorial be celebrated in history without interruption until Christ's glorious return (1 Cor. 11:26)."[39]

This mandate establishes an essential inner unity between the mission of Christ and the mission of the Church. The mandate of Christ also establishes the Church, through the priesthood of the apostles and their successors, as the sole means by which God's salvation extends forward in history. This salvation, which is the expression of God's love, is communicated through the Church liturgically, sacramentally. In the Church's "solemn remembrance, *the means of salvation history*—the death and resurrection of the Lord—is truly present."[40]

Recognition of the original integral relation of Word and sacrament is the final piece of Benedict's historical reconstruction of early Christianity. Once more we see how, in Benedict's vision, the Church's self-understanding and its structures grow naturally from its encounter with Christ. We also see again the "Word-centeredness" of his vision. The faith that the Word calls us to is faith in the Word proclaimed and heard in the Church. This faith, in turn, must be expressed in a word of faith expressed in the sacramental context of baptism—"a word about the Word"—a word by which we hand ourselves over to this Word, giving up our individual "I" to enter into communion with Christ and the whole Church.

> Paul furnishes us with a remarkable and extremely helpful statement on this matter when he says that faith is an obedience "from the heart to the form of doctrine into which you were handed over" (Rom. 6:17). These words ultimately express the sacramental character of faith, the intrinsic connection between confession and sacrament. The apostle says that a "form of doctrine" is an essential component of faith. We do not think up faith on our own. It does not come *from* us as an idea of ours but *to* us as a word from outside. It is, as it were, a word about the Word; we are "handed

39. General Audience (April 26, 2006).
40. *Principles*, 26; emphasis added. See also *Ecumenism*, 8.

over" *into* this Word that reveals new paths to our reason and gives form to our life.

We are "handed over" into the Word that precedes us through an immersion in the water symbolizing death. . . . To be handed over into the doctrine is to be handed over into Christ. We cannot receive his Word as a theory in the same way that we learn, say, mathematical formulas or philosophical opinions. We can learn it only in accepting a share in Christ's destiny. But we can become sharers in Christ's destiny only where he has permanently committed himself to sharing in man's destiny: in the Church. In the language of the Church we call this event a "sacrament." The act of faith is unthinkable without the sacramental component. . . . In another passage, Paul calls this form of doctrine a confession (compare Rom. 10:9). A further aspect of the faith event thus emerges. That is, the faith that comes to us as a Word must also become a word in us, a word that is simultaneously the expression of our life. To believe is always also to confess the faith. Faith is not private but something public that concerns the community. The Word of faith first enters the mind, but it cannot stay there: thought must always become word and deed again.[41]

This is what happens in baptism, which is a matter of professing faith in the Word of the Church in the context of the sacramental liturgy. We do not baptize ourselves but come to the Church for baptism, to profess the word of faith ("a word about the Word") in the presence of the community of those who have already bound themselves to live by faith in this Word.[42] This profession takes the form of a sacrament in which we internalize and become one with the Word. In embracing the divine Word in faith, we give ourselves over to this Word, permitting it to become the form of our lives.[43]

41. *Catechism*, 29–31.

42. "To become a Christian is to enter into this one particular Creed, into the communal form of the faith. The inner bond between the community itself and this Creed is expressed by the fact that the acceptance into the community has the form of a sacrament: baptism and catechesis are inseparable. . . . By its very nature, the word of faith presupposes the community that lives it, that is bound to it, and adheres to it in its very power to bind mankind" (*Principles*, 329–30).

43. *Catechism*, 30–31; *Principles*, 26; *Theology*, 52.

The Creed as Authoritative Interpretation of Scripture

The communal, sacramental celebration of baptism recognizes the historical and ecclesial character of conversion, that is, that the faith of the Church necessarily precedes every individual believer's faith and is the instrument by which individuals come to the faith. Profession of the Creed, as Benedict notes, has always been preceded by a period of *catechumenate*, or instruction in the Word and in the truths of the faith.[44] Hence he says, "Whenever we talk about the Word of God, we mean also to include the Creed, which stands at the heart of the process of baptism; the Creed is the way in which the Church accepts and appropriates the Word."[45]

Benedict notes that many of the Church's doctrines and dogmas originally arose in the context of catechesis. Here he notices too the centrality of the Word and the integral relationship of the Church's doctrines and the sacred Scriptures. The Church's Creed, doctrines, and dogmas, he says, are "nothing other than [the] interpretation of Scripture."[46]

As with the other essential elements of the tradition, the Creed is an expression of the Spirit of Christ present in the Church. In the creeds the Spirit explains the Old Testament in light of the Christ-event. Benedict notices also that the confession of faith itself, the *symbol* or Creed, represents an interpretive synthesis of the biblical testimony by which the Church determined "what actually constituted Christianity."[47] The symbol presumes an understanding of history as one of salvation in which Christ and the Church are the fulfillment of God's salvific promises to the children of Abraham, the people of Israel. In this, the symbol confirms the apostolic decision to join into one canon the Old Testament of Israel and the New Testament of Christ.

This is an important finding. What Benedict helps us to see is how the original Christian confession of faith is established on a

44. "Hand in hand with the sign there was always the instruction, the Word, that gave the sign its place in the history of Israel's covenant with God" (*Principles*, 29).

45. *Pilgrim*, 142.

46. Joseph Ratzinger, "Sources and Transmission of the Faith," *Communio* 10, no. 1 (1983): 20.

47. *Principles*, 149.

belief in the unity of Scripture that reflects a prior unity of history. In the confession of faith, we also find the principle of interpretation by which we are to read and understand the meaning of the Scriptures and of history.

In its simplest form, the Christian confession is summarized in the name "Jesus Christ." In this confession, Jesus, the historical figure whose life and deeds are recorded in the New Testament, is acknowledged to be the "Christ," that is, the anointed Messiah foretold in the Old Testament.[48] Here again in the original constitution of Christian life there is an essential continuity with the faith of Israel. To accept Christ as Israel's Messiah through sacramental baptism and the confession of faith is to join one's personal history to that of the family history of Israel. "To become a Christian means entering into the history of faith that began with Abraham and, thus, accepting him as father."[49]

We also see once again the correlation of creed, canon, and cult. The confession of faith in Jesus Christ, made in the sacramental-liturgical context, reveals that "Christian identity . . . is founded on the unity of the testaments."[50] This confession, in turn, is the interpretive hinge for understanding the Bible and history; we can now view both in light of the saving work of Christ in his cross and resurrection. The creedal statements and confessions of the early Church, produced by councils of the apostles' successors, demonstrate concretely the inseparability of Word, authority, and liturgy in the establishment of the Church. They also point us to the crucial role of theology in helping the Church to understand and articulate the deposit of faith.

Benedict's historical study exposes the false premises of the project of "de-Hellenization," which we explored in the last chapter and will take up again in the next chapter. Benedict often points to the example of the Council of Nicaea's use of the Greek philosophical word *homoousios* to express the divinity of Christ. The term, a "purely philosophical and certainly not biblical word," means literally that Jesus Christ is "of one being" with God. The product of much theological speculation and debate, the term

48. "Revelation," 37; *Principles*, 183.
49. *Truth*, 97.
50. *Religions*, 18.

was finally settled on to clarify the Gospel testimony that Jesus
Christ was the only-begotten Son of the Father. The religions of
the non-Christian world spoke mythologically about the sons of
the gods, but the Christians believed that Jesus was God's Son in
a way that was "real," not in the sense of an image or a flight of
poetic exaggeration. Nor did they consider Jesus to be an "avatar"
or a manifestation of the Divinity. But just what precisely was the
Church claiming about Jesus?

> *Homoousios* answers this question. It is saying: The word "Son" is
> not meant poetically or allegorically (or mythologically, symboli-
> cally), but quite realistically. That is what Jesus *is* in reality; that is
> not just what he is being called. The realism of biblical faith is being
> defended, that is all; the reality and seriousness of event, of what
> happens, of what comes in from outside. In this "is," there is the
> echo of the "I am" used in the burning bush (Exod. 3:14), whatever
> its historical origin and significance may have been. Jesus said more
> than once, "I am" and thereby expressed all the realism of the biblical
> faith; the expression in the Creed . . . is just telling us in the end that
> we can take the Bible at its word, that in its ultimate assertions it is
> literally, and not just allegorically, true. In deciding this the Fathers
> very clearly grasped that the Bible was not just meaning to introduce
> some kind of "orthopraxy." It lays claim to something more. It re-
> gards man as being able to recognize truth and means to confront
> him with truth itself, to open for him the truth that stands before
> men as a person in Jesus Christ. The distinguishing mark of Greek
> philosophy was that it did not rest content with traditional religions
> or with the images of the myths; rather, in all seriousness, it put the
> question about truth. So perhaps at this point we may be able to
> recognize the hand of providence—why the encounter between the
> faith of the Bible and Greek philosophy was truly "providential."[51]

Toward a Hermeneutic of Faith

We are now in a position to summarize and appraise Benedict's
account of Christian origins. Benedict posits an original inte-

51. *Truth*, 94–95. See also *Jesus*, 320.

gral and inseparable unity of Church and Word. He has demonstrated that this linkage is not theoretical or hypothetical but rather reflects historical circumstances and developments in the early Church. He has established that the original institutions of the Church—the canon of Scripture, the apostolic succession and tradition, and the rule of faith—were interrelated and ordered to the sacramental liturgy and mission of the Church. Finally, he has established that everything in the Church can be understood as a response to the encounter with the Word of God, believed to be made flesh in Jesus Christ.

Based on his historical study, it is incontrovertible that "in the ancient Church, the reading of Scripture and the confession of faith were primarily liturgical acts of the whole assembly gathered around the Risen Lord."[52] Moreover, we can say that the Word of God in the Church is the gateway to the sacraments; hence catechesis in the ancient Church was called "*mystagogy*, preparing the way to baptism and to the process of conversion."[53]

Benedict demonstrates at every turn that, contrary to the assertive presumptions of historical criticism, the Church's structures of authority, doctrine, and liturgy are *not* historical addenda overlaying or imposed on the Scriptures; rather, these structures are historically constituitive dimensions of the Word. As such, he calls into question modern exegesis's methodological suspicion of the Church's "interference" with the presumably pure original Word of Scripture. Without these ecclesial structures, as Benedict shows, there would in fact be no Scripture. He also makes a compelling case on historical grounds that the Scriptures cannot be adequately understood apart from the Church and its mission and liturgy.

As we turn to consider his understanding of the theological task and then to his own theology, this order needs to be kept in mind. Benedict's historical recovery is just that—it is *historical*, not theological. He is recovering what actually happened and how and why these things happened in the life of the early Church. He

---

52. *Principles*, 150.
53. Joseph Ratzinger, "Introduction to *The Catechism of the Catholic Church*," in *Introduction to* The Catechism of the Catholic Church, Joseph Cardinal Ratzinger and Christoph Schönborn (San Francisco: Ignatius, 1994), 29.

does not read his own theological presuppositions back into early Church history. Instead, he shows how the Church's theological assumptions grew organically out of its historical encounter with the Word of God.

We also need to keep in mind Benedict's primary concerns, which he describes as "scientific." As we said at the outset, Benedict is looking for the framework of biblical interpretation that holds the most "explanatory power." From the standpoint of science, as he explains, the legitimacy of such a framework depends on how well it respects and preserves the original integrity of the Scriptures without imposing its own preconceptions or otherwise interfering with the texts. His proposed alternative to the exclusive use of the historical-critical method is the "hermeneutic of faith." Unlike the historical-critical method, which originated in modern philosophy and epistemology, this hermeneutic grows organically out of Benedict's reflection on the data gained from scientific historical study of the Scriptures themselves—the data we have examined above. As we will see, his hermeneutic of faith, which culminates in a profound biblical theology, cannot be painted as some kind of slavish return to the "old ways" of the ancient Church. It represents instead a deep apprehension of the inner logic and necessity of reading from the heart of the Church.

4

The Spiritual Science of Theology

Its Mission and Method in the Life of the Church

The Original Unity between the Word and the Church

Benedict's theological project involves the faithful search for understanding of the God who has revealed himself to the world in Jesus Christ. This search drives Benedict's efforts to purify the historical-critical method and his efforts to recover the ancient form of the Church. In his critique of criticism he wants to define the legitimate limits of the method. In this he is reacting to the tendency in the last century to exalt historical criticism as the "sole scientific way" of reading the Bible. By identifying procedural prejudices and blind spots, his aim is not to discredit the method but to open it to new possibilities of fruitful inquiry and understanding. As we have seen, Benedict undertakes his critique with full respect for the goals of science, which seeks to produce theories that have the greatest explanatory power in terms of the phenomena it studies.

Alongside his reevaluation of modern critical methods, we have also observed Benedict's attempt to reappropriate the essential shape of primitive Christianity. He seeks to recover this shape as the normative criteria for understanding the nature and practice of theology and biblical interpretation in the Church. This effort should not be viewed as a kind of "primitivist" turn or "back-to-the-basics" movement. Benedict's return to the sources is, on the one hand, an act of solidarity with the founding figures of early Christianity and a search for the living Spirit and true form of the faith. But on the other hand, it also has a clear scientific intention and character. Benedict believes that if we want to come up with theological, hermeneutical, and exegetical methods that have genuine explanatory power, we need to know where Scripture came from, how it was formed, and what were its original intention and function. Such questions, as we saw in the preceding chapter, necessarily lead us to reflect on the nature of the Church, in which the Scriptures originated and have been handed on.

Benedict's theological and exegetical work, then, is rooted in a kind of *ressourcement*, that is, a historical retrieval of the original structure of God's revelation in the Church.[1] And as we will see, his interpretive suppositions and methods flow from the original integral relationship that he finds between the Church and the Word of God. As we have already suggested, Benedict does not primarily understand the Church institutionally or in terms of bureaucratic forms of authority and organization. The Church is, as the Greek word *ecclesia* implies, a gathering together, a response to the summons of the Word of God.

> Her form is the incarnate Word of God that is made flesh again and again by the Word of faith and, as flesh deigns again and again to become Word. Or, more exactly, the content of the "coming together" is the receiving of the Word of God, which reaches its climax in the remembrance of the death of Jesus, in a remembrance that creates presence and signifies mission.[2]

It is beyond our purposes here to discuss in depth Benedict's ecclesiology. We need simply to acknowledge that for him the

1. For Benedict's appreciation of the *ressourcement* movement in theology, see *Principles*, 133–34.
2. *Principles*, 352.

Church is the body of Christ, the people of God, and the liturgical-sacramental *communio* of God and humanity. The Church is the people of God gathered in faith by Christ, the Incarnate Word, who continues to communicate himself in the preaching, teaching, and sacramental ministry of his apostolic successors, thereby giving us his body and blood and making us one body in the communion of God and man.[3] The Church originates from and is perpetuated in dialogue with the divine Word, which gives the Church its "identity and continuity." In turn, the Church becomes the source by which the Word is preserved and proclaimed in the world.[4]

This relationship sets up a reciprocal dialogic of divine revelation and human response in the form of worship (*leitourgia*) and service (*diakonia*). All of the Church's work, including the work of theology and exegesis, is understood to be a response to its formative encounter with the Word, or the self-communication of God as creative Reason or *Logos*. The revelation of the hidden purposes of God's will for history that occurred in the Incarnation is a response to the deepest needs of God's creatures, whom he created with an inner thirst for truth and love. The dialogue of God and man in the Church is an essential concept for Benedict. Surveying the development of Christian anthropology, he writes, "the Bible with its phenomenon of the God who speaks, the God who is *in* dialogue, stimulated the concept of the 'person.'"[5] The encounter with Scripture is indeed the encounter with "the God who speaks dialogically." This dialogical relationship puts the human person into a "partnership" with God by which the person is "called by God to love in the world."[6] In this relationship, this partnership, the meaning of human personhood comes to light. The meaning of human personhood is transformed and fulfilled in the Incarnation. The dynamic of the divine-human dialogue reaches its dramatic climax as God speaks, not by prophets

3. *Communion*, 32, 37; *Pilgrim*, 77; "Revelation," 29.
4. *Pilgrim*, 33.
5. Joseph Ratzinger, "Concerning the Notion of Person in Theology," *Communio* 17, no. 3 (1990): 443. This essay is not often cited in the scholarly literature on Benedict, but it should be; it represents a major meditation and appropriation of the patristic tradition and has many implications for the study of early Christian exegesis and for understanding the development of Christian anthropology.
6. Ratzinger, "Notion of Person," 443.

or messengers, but by the Son and heir through whom he created the world (cf. Heb. 1:1–2). The purpose of the Incarnation is proclaimed and effected in the sacramental ministry of the Church. There the Word made flesh in Jesus is definitively revealed to be not only informative, giving us abstract knowledge of God, but also *performative*.[7] Through the Church's sacramental ministry the Word brings about the reality of which it speaks, namely, the experience of communion with the love of God.

The Church, then, is missionary and liturgical by its origin and its nature. It exists to proclaim God's loving presence in history and to cause the communion of all men and women with the divine will, joining them through the sacraments to the covenants of promise first made to Israel thousands of years ago and now given to all nations through the Church until the end of the age and the return of Christ.

There is an essential unity, as Benedict sees it, between Christ and the Church and between the Word and the Church. The connection is the *successio apostolorum*, which by its nature and by its ministry is *sacramental*, continuing Christ's work and effectuating his abiding presence in the world. "In other words, [the Church] carries forward that dialogical structure that pertains to the essence of revelation."[8]

The Dialogue of Church and Word

Theology springs from this dialogue between the Church and the Word. It begins in a faithful listening to the Word that speaks to the Church and is, ultimately, the attempt to understand this Word. As such, "theology presupposes faith" in the Word that is given.[9] Theology flows from the natural desire to better know the One we have come to believe in, namely, the God who has shown his face to us in Jesus Christ. Thus Benedict can say: "The reve-

7. Pope Benedict XVI, *Spe Salvi*, Encyclical Letter on Christian Hope (November 30, 2007), 2, 4, 10.
    8. *Communion*, 120. See also *Pilgrim*, 64.
    9. *Pilgrim*, 32. See also *Theology*, 55.

lation of Christ is . . . the fundamental normative starting point for theology."[10] Belief in that revelation, that is, conversion to the Word that reveals, is likewise prerequisite to the theological task. The theologian must first pronounce his or her own word of faith through the sacrament of baptism, entering into the faith of the Church that always precedes his or her own faith and accepting the Word and pledging to order his or her life according to it.

As theology flows from the act of faith, theology by its nature shares in the Church's mission of proclamation of and witness to the Word. Benedict follows what he describes as St. Bonaventure's twofold justification of theology. In the first place, theology is a response to the command of 1 Peter 3:15: "Always be ready to make your defense (*apologian*) to anyone who demands from you an accounting (*logon*) for the hope that is in you." This passage shows the nature of faith to be something that is not a private decision but rather "wishes to make itself understandable to others." Again, before the faith can be communicated, it must be interiorized. It must become the inner Word (*logos*) that guides the innermost being of the believer. "The *logos* must be so intimately their own that it can become *apo-logia*; through the mediation of Christians, the Word [*Wort*] becomes response [*Antwort*] to man's questions."[11]

Faith in Christ, in this view, possesses an inner dynamism that orients believers toward the desire to know the truth about this God in whom they believe and to understand as fully as possible his Word to them. But, again following Bonaventure, Benedict sees faith as also partaking of "the dynamism of love," which impels the believer to seek to know the God he or she loves with ever-greater intimacy.[12]

> Faith can wish to understand because it is moved by love for the One upon whom it has bestowed its consent. Love seeks understanding. It wishes to know ever better the one whom it loves. It "seeks his

10. Pope Benedict XVI, Address to Members of the International Theological Commission (December 1, 2005).

11. *Theology*, 26.

12. *Theology*, 104.

face," as Augustine never tires of repeating. Love is the desire for intimate knowledge, so that the quest for intelligence can even be an inner requirement of love. Put another way, there is a coherence of love and truth which has important consequences for theology and philosophy. Christian faith can say of itself, I have found love. Yet love for Christ and of one's neighbor for Christ's sake can enjoy stability and consistency only if its deepest motivation is love for the truth. This adds a new aspect to the missionary element: real love of neighbor also desires to give him the deepest thing man needs, namely, knowledge and truth.[13]

The "Ecclesial" Nature and Mission of Theology

We see that for Benedict, theology is far from a private affair. Theology is "ecclesial" by nature.[14] It flows from the Word that calls one to faith in the Church. It is a reflection on that Word heard in the Church and that resounds in the depths of one's own soul. And it is always *for* the Church; that is, the work of theology is always in the service of the Church's mission. As an expression of the Church's faith, theology carries a "missionary dynamism" that naturally orients it to preaching and catechesis—to leading others to the encounter with the Word, to communion in the family of God.[15]

This is not to reduce the work of theology to apologetics or catechetics. Indeed, Benedict sees theology's missionary impulse as issuing from the heart of the Christian faith experience. The innate character of faith, which is a summons to the love of God and neighbor, impels every believer to seek a deeper understanding and love of God, not only for oneself, but also for one's neighbor. If we believe the testimony of the Word, that in Jesus resides the truth about human history and happiness, then love for our neighbor will lead us to testify to that Word. Theology is ordered to this testimony, which is part of the proclamation and teaching

13. *Theology*, 27.
14. Address to Members of the International Theological Commission (December 1, 2005); *Theology*, 105.
15. *Theology*, 27.

of the Church: "to tell man who he is and . . . to disclose to him the truth about himself, that is, what he can base his life on and what he can die for."[16]

Theology, then, is a part of the Church's "living transmission" of the faith, bound up integrally with the tradition founded on the apostles' teaching and prayer, "which interprets the Word which is handed down and gives it an unequivocal clarity of meaning."[17] Here we again observe the organic characteristic of Benedict's thought. He does not propose or impose his own ideas about theology. Rather, his thoughts on the nature and mission of theology naturally grow out of his reflections on the historical nature and mission of the Church.

As a result of this natural connection, Benedict rejects the modern presumption that there is a necessary tension between the work of theology and the teaching mission of the Church. Present-day controversies are rooted in the problems he identifies in his critique of criticism, namely, an overreaching application of "scientific" and rational methods and an unwarranted hermeneutic of suspicion that presumes a dialectical opposition between the "institutional Church" and the gospel.

To presume a conflict between theology and the Church is to misunderstand the historical relationship between theology and the Church and between the Church's preaching and its teaching, at least as those two aspects of its mission are reflected in the Scriptures. The Church is "the ground of theology's existence and the condition which makes it possible."[18] Always and fundamentally, Benedict insists that "theology is interpretation."[19] That is, the theologian does not properly begin with his own ideas. "Theology is pondering what God has said and thought before us."[20]

Nor, as we have indicated, is theology an isolated task of the individual. Theology is always corporate, always ecclesial. It begins in the Church and flows from the act of faith in the Word that has been

16. *Theology*, 63–64.
17. *Theology*, 60.
18. *Theology*, 61.
19. *Theology*, 93.
20. *Theology*, 103–4. See also *Principles*, 325–27.

given. The task of a truly Christian theology cannot be conceived apart from the Church's faith in the Word that is given by God and preserved and proclaimed in the Church in history. We do not come to the faith without the Church. We believe only because we have heard the Word that speaks to us from the heart of the Church and have accepted that Word as the norm for our lives in the sacramental waters of baptism. The Word that speaks with such authority as to compel us to believe is the same Word that theology seeks to understand, reflect on, and interpret. And the Church that proclaims that Word with authority likewise is entrusted to care for this Word, to protect it from manipulation and misinterpretation.

> The path of theology is indicated by the saying, "*Credo ut intelligam*" [Faith seeks understanding]: I accept what is given in advance, in order to find, starting from this and in this, the path to the right way of living, to the right way of understanding myself. Yet that means that theology, of its nature, presupposes *auctoritas*. . . . This authority is a Word. . . . The Word comes from understanding and is intended to lead to understanding.[21]

From these reflections, it is clear that the Church's teaching authority, its magisterium, cannot be regarded as an extraneous or "foreign" element that constricts the freedom of the theologian. The authority of the Church over the Word is part of the essential historical structure of God's revelation in the Church. As we observed in the previous chapter, historically speaking, Scripture, tradition, and the Church's apostolic teaching authority are inseparable facets of the same reality, namely, the revelation of the Word to the Church.[22] The authority of the Church as "the primary interpreter of the Word" is the *auctoritas apostolica*—the authority of the living Word communicated as *viva vox*, as the living voice of the apostolic preaching. The Church's preaching, its proclamation of the faith, is quite naturally "the normative criterion of theology" because this proclamation, the gospel the Church proclaims, is the very "object of theological reflection."

21. *Pilgrim*, 31, 35. See also *Theology*, 45.
22. *Pilgrim*, 36.

The Church is called to preach, not to teach "scientific theology," Benedict insists. But the ministry of preaching and the ministry of theology share in the common mission of the Church.[23] This does not sentence theology to the slavish repetition of Church dogmas. In fact, as we will see in Benedict's theology, the Church's dogmas, teachings, and liturgy become key avenues of insight, opening the way for new and creative interpretations of the divine Word.

The Spiritual Science of the Normative Theologians

We see the further implications of the historical "interwovenness" of Church and Word in Benedict's discussion of the nature and mission of theology. Theology, as reconstructed by Benedict according to its original place in the primitive Church, is an ecclesial work that always seeks to help the Church understand the divine Word and articulate the truths of the faith in terms of the questions and challenges of its own time and culture.[24]

We are now in the position to begin to make some summary judgments and conclusions. It is important to keep in mind that Benedict does not give us a theological system. He gives us instead an illuminating pathway that helps us to think through both what theology *is* in the Church and how theology might better proceed in order to be effective. In the discussion that follows, we must anticipate something that will become clearer when we turn to consider Benedict's own biblical theology. That is, for Benedict there is a high degree of correspondence between theology and biblical interpretation. Keeping this in mind, let us consider what I take to be Benedict's most daring and fertile assertion of methodological principle in theology:

> Theology is a spiritual science. The normative theologians are the authors of Holy Scripture. This statement is valid not only with reference to the objective written document they left behind but

---

23. *Theology*, 63, 97, 104. Cf. *Co-Workers*, 40: "But the ministry of proclamation is likewise the ministry of theology."

24. Pope Benedict XVI, Address to Lenten Meeting with the Clergy of Rome (February 22, 2007).

also with reference to their manner of speaking, in which it is God himself who speaks. I think this fact has great significance for our present situation.[25]

This important programmatic statement needs to be parsed closely in order for us to understand first what Benedict means by theology and later what he is up to in his theology. He says: Theology is *a spiritual science*. Theology is the scientific study of things of the Spirit—it is ultimately about God, who is Spirit (John 4:24). So the first point to be clarified is that theology is about God. God is the ultimate subject of theology. Theology seeks to understand the God who reveals himself in his Word to the Church. As such, theology is "rational reflection upon God's revelation."[26]

Of course, God has done more than deliver a collection of texts to the Church. The Word has been made flesh in Jesus Christ. Following the normative theologians of the New Testament, Benedict posits that the "content" of theology is always reflection on the meaning of the life, death, and resurrection of Jesus Christ. The New Testament, after all, is "about" Jesus Christ, that is, who he is, the full meaning of the salvation-historical event of his resurrection, and how his presence remains in the world through his Church.[27] Theology for Benedict is essentially Christology. It takes as its starting point the Christ-event and most decisively the event of the resurrection. Hence Benedict writes: "All Christian theology, if it is to be true to its origin, must be first and foremost a theology of resurrection."[28] The primary data for theology remains the words and deeds of Jesus as remembered and interpreted in the New Testament.[29]

This presupposition about theology is based on the prior assumption of the reliability of Scripture as the authentically divine Word. This assumption goes well beyond what can be "proven" by scientific means. But theology is not philosophy, which inquires

25. *Principles*, 321–22.
26. *Theology*, 16.
27. *Way*, 76–77.
28. *Principles*, 184–85.
29. "The remembrance and retention of the words of Jesus and of the course of his life, especially his passion, were from the beginning an essential factor in the formation of Christian tradition and in the norms applied to it" (*Dogma*, 4).

into metaphysical or spiritual realities solely by rational methods. Theology is a *spiritual science*. Theology proceeds according to rational *and* spiritual means, according to a hermeneutic of faith that guides our inquiry. And we conduct this inquiry by the rational principles and methods of the human sciences. Just as one cannot learn how to swim without being in water, one cannot do theology without "the spiritual praxis" of the life of faith.[30] Faith is essential to the theological task. But so is reason.

To say that theology is a spiritual science is to say that "faith and rational reflection are integral to theology. The absence of either principle would bring about theology's demise."[31] In order to be authentically Christian, the work of theology must proceed according to the harmonious effort of faith and reason. This is no arbitrary diktat imposed from outside; this principle flows from the basic structure of revelation and the faith.

Conversion and the Act of Faith: Prerequisite to Theology

As Benedict sees it, theology must be an expression of conversion and discipleship. Theology is faith seeking to understand the "contents" of the faith, that is, the revelation of God in Jesus Christ to the people of God, the Church. It follows that theology must begin with a faith commitment, a conversion to Jesus Christ. Taking the New Testament authors as "normative" means, in the first place, that the theologian must be a person who has heard and believed the Word, professed his or her faith by being baptized into the Church, and committed to living according to the Church's moral and sacramental norms.

The New Testament authors were believers in Jesus, and their writings stem from the act of faith and the experience of following Jesus in faith. The theologians of the New Testament presume that knowledge of Christ and his gospel comes only to those who follow him as disciples.[32]

---

30. *Principles*, 322.
31. *Theology*, 57.
32. "In biblical language: in order to know Christ, it is necessary to follow him. Only then do we know where he lives" (*Way*, 67). See also *Principles*, 323.

Because there is no theology without faith, there can be no theology without conversion. Conversion can take many forms. . . . In one form or another, however, the convert must consciously pronounce in his own name a Yes to this new beginning and really turn from the "I" to the "no-longer-I." It is thus immediately obvious that the opportunity for creative theology increases the more that faith becomes real, personal experience; the more that conversion acquires interior certainty thanks to a painful process of transformation; the more that it is recognized as the indispensable means of penetrating into the truth of one's own being. This is why in every age the path to faith can take its bearings by converts; it explains why they in particular can help us to recognize the reason for the hope that is in us (cf. 1 Pet. 3:15) and to bear witness to it. The connection between faith and theology is not, therefore, some sort of sentimental or pietistic twaddle but is a direct consequence of the logic of the thing and is corroborated by the whole of history.[33]

As he puts it here in no uncertain terms, Benedict does not envision the hermeneutic of faith as an excuse for lazy or unscientific theology. As we saw in the last chapter, faith for Benedict is far more than pious acceptance of specific assertions and events. Faith, like reason, is *a way of knowing.*[34]

We will explore this point more fully in the next chapter, where we will examine Benedict's beliefs about the historical reliability of the Scriptures in general and the Gospels in particular. Here it is important to note that the act of faith gives the theologian the power to accept the Scriptures as the Word of God and the Church as the people of God in whom the Scriptures remain a living Word.[35] This acceptance of the Church as the living subject of Scripture is vital for Benedict's approach to theology. He has expressed this with almost axiom-like clarity:

For the Catholic Christian, two lines of essential hermeneutic orientation assert themselves. . . . The first: we trust Scripture and we base ourselves on Scripture, not on hypothetical reconstructions

33. *Theology*, 57.
34. "Magisterium"; emphasis added.
35. *Benedict XVI*, 145; *Jesus*, xx–xxi.

that go behind it and, according to their own taste, reconstruct a history in which the presumptuous idea of our knowing what can or cannot be attributed to Jesus plays a key role; which, of course, means attributing to him only what a modern scholar is happy to attribute to a man belonging to a time that the scholar himself has reconstructed. The second is that we read Scripture in the living community of the Church, and therefore on the basis of the fundamental decisions thanks to which it has become historically efficacious, namely, those that laid the foundations of the Church. One must not separate the text from this living context. In this sense, Scripture and Tradition form an inseparable whole, and it is this that Luther, at the dawn of the awakening of historical awareness, could not see.[36]

Theology, as a spiritual science, a science conducted by the Christian believer, is an *ecclesial* science. The normative theologians were believers joined in one body by baptism in the Church. The purpose of their theologizing was to understand the content of their faith and to fulfill the command of Christ: that they make disciples of all nations.

The Church: The Living Subject of Theology

The Church, then, for Benedict is the living context in which the spiritual science of theology is performed. Against the hypothetical historical reconstructions of modern critics, Benedict asserts the actual historical foundations of the Church. He demonstrates that Scripture and all the various facets of the Church's tradition—its teachings, prayers, sacraments, saints, and interpretive traditions— came to be in response to the Word of God.

The Scripture emerged from within the heart of a living subject—the pilgrim people of God—and lives within this same subject. . . . The People of God—the Church—is the living subject of Scripture; it is in the Church that the words of the Bible are always in the present. This also means, of course, that the People has to receive its very

36. *Benedict XVI*, 145.

self from God, ultimately from the incarnate Christ; it has to let itself be ordered, guided, and led by him.[37]

This means that theology, too, as interpretive reflection on this deposit of faith, grows out of the theologian's experience as a member of this pilgrim people, this family of God created by the Incarnation. As we did not make up the faith on our own but came to believe in the prior faith of the Church, so also we cannot do theology apart from "this living subject in which the Word lives."[38]

Benedict believes that the Word, as a divine Word, cannot be understood today unless it is apprehended in light of "the diversity of an interpretation that develops for thousands of years." The words of the human authors "become God's Word only in the unity of Scripture as whole in the living subject of the people of God."[39] The meaning of this Word grows in various rereadings and interpretations given to it as the pilgrim family of God makes its way through history in conversation with God. The meaning of this conversation, which is the subject of theology, cannot be fully grasped except in the light of the full "reciprocity of God's call and the human response."[40]

This reciprocity of divine Word and the human response constitutes the whole tradition of the Church. The data that theology interprets is never simply the written texts. For Benedict, the Reformation principle of *sola Scriptura* is neither sufficient for theology nor consistent with the "inner structure" of the Word as it has been given to us historically in the Church. Simply stated, the Word of God did not begin as a "book," a fact modern criticism has proved. Benedict grants that the Word and the Church's

37. *Jesus*, xx–xxi.

38. Pope Benedict XVI, Address to Meeting with the Youth of Rome and the Lazio Region in Preparation for World Youth Day (April 6, 2006). We will develop this notion of the inspiration and interpretive history of the Word in the next chapter.

39. Pope Benedict XVI, Address to Members of the Roman Clergy (March 2, 2006); *Jesus*, xx.

40. Pope Benedict XVI, Address to the Community of the Roman Major Seminary on the Occasion of the Feast of Our Lady of Trust (February 17, 2007).

proclamation of the Word in its preaching and teaching should always be the "measure" of theology, that is, the criteria by which the adequacy of theological formulations is to be judged. Indeed, the content of the Church's proclamation is the subject matter for theology.[41]

But the Word that theology seeks to understand is always more than the written Word of sacred Scripture. To refer back to Benedict's programmatic statement about normative theology, we see that the "written document . . . left behind" by the normative theologians of the New Testament bears witness to this. This normative document, for Benedict, testifies that "the Bible is the condensation of a process of Revelation which is much greater and inexhaustible. . . . It is then part of a living organism which, through the vicissitudes of history, nonetheless conserves its identity and which, as a result, can, so to speak, claim its 'rights of authorship' from the Bible as a resource which is its own."[42]

The "book" always points us back to, among other things, the people entrusted to bear God's words and thoughts in human history.[43] "It is consequently important to read sacred Scripture and experience sacred Scripture in the communion of the Church, that is, with all the great witnesses of this Word, beginning with the first Fathers and ending with today's saints, with today's magisterium. Above all, it is a Word that becomes vital and alive in the liturgy."[44]

As we will see in the final chapters of the present book, Benedict attaches great importance to the Fathers of the Church and an even greater importance to the liturgical and sacramental dimension of the Word. The Word must always be read "in the great company of the Church, in whose liturgy these events never cease to become present anew and in which the Lord speaks with us today."[45]

41. On this, see *Theology*, 61, 63.
42. Joseph Ratzinger, "Sources and Transmission of the Faith," *Communio* 10, no. 1 (1983): 28.
43. *Jesus*, xx; *Principles*, 329.
44. Address to the Community of the Roman Major Seminary (February 17, 2007).
45. Address to Meeting with the Youth of Rome (April 6, 2006).

The Unity of Scripture and the "Christological Hermeneutic"

Below we will consider more fully the rational, scientific dimension of the spiritual science of theology. We see here how necessary the dimension of faith in the Church is to keeping theology from not descending into mere "historicism" or the archaeology of ancient texts. Theology must always be an act of faith made within the sacramental context of the Church. There must be a connection with the life of the Church, which is a connection with Christ himself and with the beginnings of the Church.[46]

The faith of the Church, as the people of God, gives the Bible its unity, integrity, and continuity. And the Word of revelation can be understood only in light of this profound unity given to it by the living subject of the Church. The unity of Scripture in a single canon is something that can be grasped only by faith. This is one crucial weakness in relying exclusively on the tools of historical criticism to interpret the Bible. With these tools one is limited to studying "the individual books of Scripture in the context of their historical period, and then analyzing them further according to their sources." Such critical study is essential, but without reference to the faith of the Church, it can yield only separate hypotheses about individual texts. Its conclusions can only leave us in the past. It cannot provide us with interpretations that make sense within the totality of Scripture.[47]

> The faith of the Church does not exist as an ensemble of texts, rather, the texts—the words—exist because there is a corresponding subject which gives them their basis and their inner coherence. . . . In this regard, the basic tension between the Old and New Testaments already indicates to what an extent the truth of the faith can become accessible in language only within the inner coherence of the whole, and not in separate propositions. If one strikes out the continuity of a subject which organically traverses the whole of history and which remains one with itself throughout its own transformations, nothing

46. Joseph Ratzinger, "Cardinal Frings's Speeches during the Second Vatican Council: Apropos of A. Muggeridge's *The Desolate City,*" *Communio* 15, no. 1 (1988): 137.

47. *Jesus,* xvii.

is left beyond contradictory speech fragments which cannot subsequently be brought into any relation. The tendency to search for what is most ancient and original behind present developments is the logical conclusion of the loss of the binding element which holds history together and unifies it in the midst of its contradictions. Theology becomes archeology and busies itself with exhuming the authentic ideal behind what really appears before our eyes as Christianity. Such reconstructed Christianity, however, is always a selective Christianity, which loses the tension and the wealth of the whole. The disjointed pluralism of subjectively minted selective Christianities comes to replace the inner plurality of the symphony of the faith.[48]

As the living subject of theology, the Church testifies to the unity of God's revelation. In a material sense, that unity is expressed in the biblical canon, which unites the Old and New Testaments into a single book. The unity of the canon is an essential aspect of Benedict's hermeneutic of faith, as we will examine in the next chapter. So too is what he calls the "christological hermeneutic," which considers Jesus Christ and his cross and resurrection to be "the key" to understanding the Scriptures.[49]

He locates these essential elements in the work of the normative theologians. He illustrates this by reflecting on a brief statement made after Christ's cleansing of the temple as recorded in John's Gospel: "After he was raised from the dead, his disciples remembered that he had said this; and they believed the scripture and the word that Jesus had spoken" (John 2:22). The passage refers to Jesus' declaration that should his enemies destroy "this shrine," he would raise it in three days. Benedict reads this passage in light of the promise found later in John's Gospel that Jesus would send his Holy Spirit to help the disciples remember all he had said (John 14:26).

48. *Theology*, 93–95; cf. 105: "The Church, as a living subject which endures amid the changes of history, is the vital milieu of the theologian; the Church preserves faith's experiences with God. Theology can remain historically relevant only if it acknowledges this living environment, inserts itself into it and attains an inner participation . . . in the organic structure of the Church; [the theologian] needs that faith which is prayer, contemplation, and life. Only in this symphony does theology come into being."
49. *Jesus*, xix.

As Benedict reads it, we have in this passage the elements for a
biblical-theological doctrine of *memoria ecclesiae*, the Church as
memory. First, there is belief in the salvation-historical event of
the resurrection. Second, the passage reflects the Church's belief
in the unity of the Old Testament (the "Scripture" Jesus referred
them to) and the New Testament (the "word" spoken by Jesus).
Finally, there is remembrance in the Spirit, which takes place in the
ecclesial context and authority established by Jesus.[50]

We could develop Benedict's insights for theology further by
delineating more precisely the *content* of the disciples' remembrance. The "Word" that the Spirit helps the disciples remember
is in fact a spiritual or typological interpretation of the Old
Testament. In light of the resurrection and under the guidance
of the Spirit, the apostles understand Jesus' words about the
temple to have been referring to the "temple" of his body (see
John 2:21).

The passage gives us insight into Jesus' own preaching, which,
in turn, is the interpretive model followed by the apostolic writers.
As the Gospels and the other New Testament writings illustrate,
the Christian proclamation is founded on a typological or spiritual interpretation of Jesus' identity and mission in light of the
Old Testament. Benedict roots this method of interpretation in
Jesus' own teaching:

> Jesus of Nazareth claimed to be the true heir to the Old Testa-
> ment—"the Scriptures"—and to offer a true interpretation, which,
> admittedly, was not that of the schools, but came from the authority
> of the Author himself: "He taught them as one having authority,
> and not as the scribes" (Mark 1:22). The Emmaus narrative also
> expresses this claim: "Beginning with Moses and all the prophets,
> he interpreted to them the things about himself in all the Scrip-
> tures" (Luke 24:27). The New Testament authors sought to ground
> this claim in details, in particular Matthew, but Paul as well, by
> using rabbinic methods of interpretation to show that the scribal
> interpretation led to Christ as the key to the "Scriptures." For the
> authors and founders of the New Testament, the Old Testament

50. See Benedict's discussion in *Principles*, 24–25.

was simply "the Scriptures": it was only later that the developing Church gradually formed a New Testament canon which was also sacred Scripture, but in the sense that it still presupposed Israel's Bible to be such, the Bible read by the apostles and their disciples, and now called the Old Testament, which provided the interpretative key.[51]

Read through Benedict's eyes, we see the normative theologians of the New Testament in constant dialogue with the Old Testament texts. Indeed, the New Testament is described by Benedict as essentially a spiritual exegesis of the Old. "The New Testament is nothing other than an interpretation of 'the Law, the prophets, and the writings' found from or contained in the story of Jesus."[52] And, as we will see, the hallmarks of New Testament exegesis— "the internal unity of the Bible as a rule of interpretation, Christ as the meeting point of all the Old Testament pathways"[53]—are core principles of his theological and exegetical method.

Following the normative theologians, Benedict sees Christ's resurrection as a vindication of Jesus' interpretation of the Old Testament. Or, as Benedict pointedly puts it, the resurrection is "God's defense of Jesus against the official interpretation of the Old Testament as given by the competent Jewish authorities." By the resurrection, God "proves," so to speak, that Jesus is the fulfillment of the figures of the Old Testament—the suffering servant, the divine Son, and the Messiah from the line of David—as foretold by the prophets and the psalms. Of critical significance, in Benedict's mind, is the portrayal of Jesus as "the true lamb of sacrifice, the sacrifice in which the deepest meaning of all Old Testament liturgies is fulfilled." As we will see below, this has "essential significance for the Christian liturgy."[54]

As a final historical note, Benedict acknowledges that Jesus did not "invent" this way of reading the Scriptures. Already in the Old Testament, especially in the prophets and psalms, we find increasing

51. "Preface," 17.
52. Joseph Cardinal Ratzinger, *Milestones: Memoirs, 1927–1977*, trans. Erasmo Leiva-Merkiakis (San Francisco: Ignatius, 1998), 53.
53. "Preface," 14.
54. *Dogma*, 3–5.

anticipation of a messianic king who will be "the fulfilled image of the true Israel."[55] For Benedict, this intrabiblical interpretation is made possible only by faith in the Church. By faith we see the unity of God's revelation, and we see that the scriptural Word is always in the process of reinterpretation as the pilgrim Church makes its way in history.

Because of the "ecclesiality of sacred Scripture" in the journey of the Church, later Scriptures interpret earlier ones, different sections of Scripture explain one another.

> We now realize that the whole Book is a process of constantly new interpretations where one enters ever more deeply into the mystery proposed at the beginning, and that what was initially present but still closed, unfolds increasingly. In one Book, we can understand the whole journey of sacred Scripture, which is an ongoing reinterpretation, or rather, a new and better understanding of all that had been said previously.
>
> Step by step, light dawns and the Christian can grasp what the Lord said to the disciples at Emmaus, explaining to them that it was of him that all the Prophets had spoken. *The Lord unfolds to us the last re-reading*; Christ is the key to all things and only by joining the disciples on the road to Emmaus, only by walking with Christ, by reinterpreting all things in his light, with him, crucified and risen, do we enter into the riches and beauty of sacred Scripture.[56]

Vera Philosophia and the Purification of Reason by Faith

Theology is a spiritual science that begins in the act of faith made in the Church and follows the normative model of the New Testament writers. Again and again in his reconstruction of the nature and mission of theology, Benedict points us back to the dialogue with Greek philosophy and culture in which Christian theology was engaged from the start.

55. Joseph Cardinal Ratzinger, *The Meaning of Christian Brotherhood* (San Francisco: Ignatius, 1993 [1960]), 48.
56. Address to Lenten Meeting with the Clergy of Rome (February 22, 2007); emphasis added.

The Fathers of the Church, the Christian teachers in the first centuries after the apostles, are therefore very important for Benedict's reconstruction of theology. The essential continuity he sees between the New Testament Church and the era of the Fathers was demonstrated in his decision to devote his first two series of catechesis as pope to the individual apostles and to their successors, the great Christian Fathers and teachers of the faith.[57] For Benedict, the theology of the Fathers brings us close to the era of the Scriptures, "in which the waters of faith still flowed unpolluted and in all their freshness."[58]

As we will see, Benedict's own theology bears witness to the "unique union of biblical, liturgical, and theological attitudes" he finds in the Fathers.[59] But we can also detect the influence of the Fathers in his understanding of the profound union of faith and reason in the theological enterprise. The Fathers continued the encounter with culture that began in the biblical witness of St. Paul, whose preaching included quotations from Greek philosophers and poets and who incorporated philosophical concepts into his writings. This witness continues in the deep and widespread cultural engagement of the early Church Fathers, who carefully examined the philosophies, theologies, and even the entertainments of their day. And Benedict—like Paul, St. Augustine, and others—believes the Christian faith to be the *vera philosophia* and *religio vera*, the true philosophical path of enlightenment, based on the knowledge of "that divine presence which can be perceived by the rational analysis of reality."[60]

Theology's engagement with philosophy and the sciences flows also from the nature of the Word that theology seeks to interpret in faith. The Word that theology reflects on is not simply a statement of ethics or a philosophy of life. It does not claim to be an

57. See the pope's weekly General Audiences beginning March 15, 2006, and continuing into 2008. These audience talks have been collected in *The Apostles and Their Co-Workers* (Huntington, IN: Our Sunday Visitor, 2007) and *The Fathers* (Huntington, IN: Our Sunday Visitor, 2008).

58. *Principles*, 134.

59. *Principles*, 152.

60. See the discussion in *Truth*, 165–75; quote at 169.

expression of myth or an artistic, metaphoric, or symbolic word. The Word that speaks to the Church claims to be the *truth* about the objective reality of things, the way things really are. The Word claims to speak truly and authoritatively about the nature and destiny of the human, the meaning of history, the substance of what can be known and hoped for, and how we should live.

Faith gives us our starting point for the spiritual science of theology. As we discussed in considering Benedict's critique of criticism, Christian faith reveals a God who is reason (*Logos*) and love, a God who is the Creator of the universe, the ground of all being, and the foundation and source of the unity of all things.[61] But faith is not enough for us to understand and articulate this revelation, which really calls us to seek true knowledge and to affirm truths about all of reality as the creation of God's reason and love.[62] To do this we need recourse to the rational tools and disciplines that have been developed to explore and explain history, being, nature, and man; that is, we need the tools of philosophy and the other human sciences.

Theology is a spiritual science. We need to ponder the revealed Word with a reason purified by faith, because only in the profound unity of faith and reason do we preserve the human capacity for the infinite, for transcendence. We encounter at this point the fuller implications of Benedict's critique of modern reason. As we have discussed, modern reason brackets off metaphysics, claiming that nothing can be known with certainty about ultimate realities or truths. Lurking behind this "self-limitation" of reason in the search for calculable, verifiable information about the physical world is Kant's theory of knowledge.[63]

For Benedict the result is an "amputated reason," an epistemology that needlessly limits our rational thought processes to simple reflection on how things work or what we can do with things.[64] There is no justification, scientific or otherwise, to impose such limits or artificial restrictions on what we can know through reason.

61. *Truth*, 182.
62. *Pilgrim*, 291–92.
63. *Truth*, 134–35.
64. *Truth*, 158, 186.

The theory of reason that undergirds so much of contemporary theology, therefore, "does not express human reason in its fullness, but only a part of it, and because it thus mutilates reason, it cannot be considered rational."[65]

Reason can, and must, be purified. It must enlarge its scope of interest to embrace the entire range of questions that men and women have so that it "remains open to the consideration of ultimate truths."[66] Again Benedict's assumptions and assertions about the purification of reason are based on the norm observed in primitive Christianity, where the biblical authors and first Christian teachers assumed "the profound harmony of faith and reason."[67]

As we have discussed, the rationality of the world is a matter that can be and has been ascertained from both the standpoint of faith and the standpoint of reason. Our subjective reason, especially our scientific and mathematical applications of reason, prove to us that the world is objectively reasonable, that it functions according to predictable, observable patterns and laws. Divine revelation reveals the same thing: nature is reasonable. As Benedict says:

> The first item in the alphabet of faith is the statement: In the beginning was the Word. Faith reveals to us that eternal reason is the ground of all things or, put in other terms, that things are reasonable from the ground up. . . . This is what makes [faith] universal and by nature missionary. It is also the reason why faith is intrinsically "*quaerens intellectum*," as the Fathers say, that is, in search of understanding. Understanding, hence rational engagement with the priorly given Word, is a constitutive principle of the Christian faith, which of necessity spawns theology. . . .
> But what distinguishes theology from the philosophy of religion and from secular religious science? The answer is that man's reason

65. Joseph Cardinal Ratzinger, "Europe in the Crisis of Cultures," *Communio* 32, no. 2 (2005): 345–56.

66. Pope Benedict XVI, Address to Meeting with Catholic Educators (April 17, 2008).

67. Pope Benedict XVI, Homily, Washington Nationals Stadium (April 17, 2008).

knows that it has not been left to its own devices. It is preceded by a Word which, though logical and rational, does not originate from reason itself but has been granted it as a gift and, as such, always transcends it. It remains a task which we never completely fulfill in history. Theology is pondering what God has said and thought before us.[68]

Reason must be joined to faith because the Word we seek to understand, while "logical and rational," transcends our reason and confronts us as a divine gift.[69] Reason purified by faith puts us back in touch with the basis of human reason: the eternal and divine reason that is the divine *Logos*. By the act of faith, we are set free from human limitations imposed on reason.

When reason is joined with faith, we can see the world more clearly, in its greater integrity. There is a certain transparency between the physical and the spiritual, the seen and unseen, the natural and supernatural. When reason is joined to faith, our theology assumes the shape that can be noticed in early Christianity, in which "nature became transparent to the intentions of the Creator; it expresses the language of the Creator, who lets himself be perceived through creation."[70]

Normative Theology: Making Present the Word

In the chapters that follow we will see how Benedict's theology reunifies faith and reason. But before we turn to his contributions to biblical theology, we need to consider one more aspect of his theological method.

To return to his programmatic statement, he asserts starkly and potently that "the normative theologians are the authors of Holy Scripture." On the surface, he means simply that Scripture and the human authors of Scripture are meant to serve as models

68. *Theology*, 103–4. See also Address to Meeting with the Youth of Rome (April 6, 2006).
69. *Principles*, 325–27.
70. Joseph Cardinal Ratzinger, "The Renewal of Moral Theology: Perspectives of Vatican II and *Veritatis Splendor*," *Communio* 32, no. 2 (2005): 357–68.

not only for how we should "do" theology but also for what our theology should be about and how the findings of theological inquiry should be expressed. Looked at in this way, we can again see Benedict seeking normative principles and methods in the sources of the tradition, in this case in the Scriptures.

Indeed, Benedict does return to distinctions found first in ancient Greek philosophy and later in Christian appropriations of Greek philosophical categories. Aristotle, reflecting an older tradition dating back at least to Hesiod, distinguished *theología*, the divine speech of the deity, from *theologichē*, the human words produced in the effort to understand and explain the divine discourse.[71] This distinction was taken up in Christian thought by Pseudo-Dionysius and subsequently elaborated by St. Bonaventure.

In making Bonaventure's logic his own, Benedict affirms the deep encounter and synthesis of Greek philosophical thought with Christian faith in the divine inspiration of Scripture. What we call theology, according to Benedict, is closer to what Bonaventure and the ancients termed *theologichē*—our human attempts to interpret or give meaning to God's speech. What Bonaventure and Psuedo-Dionysius called "theology" or *theología* is properly reserved for sacred Scripture, for Scripture is the true speech of God, although rendered in human words.

> Properly speaking, God himself must be the subject of theology. Therefore, Scripture alone is theology in the fullest sense of the word because it truly has God as its subject; it does not just speak of him but *is* his own speech. It lets God himself speak. But Bonaventure does not thereby overlook the fact that this speaking on the part of God is, nevertheless, a human speaking. The writers of Holy Scripture speak as themselves, as men, yet, precisely in doing so, they are "*theologoi*," those through whom God as subject, as the Word that speaks itself, enters into history. What distinguishes Holy Scripture from all later theology is thus completely safeguarded, but, at the same time, the Bible becomes the model of all theology, and those who are the bearers of it become the norm of the theo-

71. *Principles*, 320–22.

logian, who accomplishes his task properly only to the extent that he makes God himself his subject.[72]

Something important is happening here. Benedict is elevating and restoring theology to its privileged position in the mission and tradition of the Church. Theology is affirmed to be more than the study of God's Word. To put it differently, God is always more than an "object" of study for theology. The theologian, following the lead of the *theologoi* of sacred Scripture, endeavors through his work to make God the living *subject* of his theology, to let God himself "speak" through his theological work.

In a way, the theologian is presented here as the handmaiden of revelation. This is a lofty duty, one requiring deep commitment of heart and mind, deep faith as well as rational and methodological rigor. As Benedict states: "Christian theology . . . is never a purely human discourse about God, but always, and inseparably, the *logos* and 'logic' of God's self-revelation. For this reason scientific rationality and lived devotion are two necessarily complementary and interdependent aspects of study."[73]

For the theologian who reads them in faith, the Scriptures are far more than ancient texts to be studied; they are the divine speech of God in human language through which we encounter the living God. The theologian, then, must approach Scripture almost in an attitude of worship.

> We have to enter into a relationship of awe and obedience toward the Bible which nowadays is frequently in danger of being lost. . . . Historical-critical exegesis can be a wonderful means for a deeper understanding of the Bible if its instruments are used with that reverent love which seeks to know God's gift in the most exact and careful way possible.[74]

Benedict's own theological work is characterized by this combination of scientific exactitude and reverent love, which sees the

72. *Principles*, 321.
73. Pope Benedict XVI, Address, Visit to Heiligenkreuz Abbey (September 9, 2007).
74. *Song*, 50.

Scriptures as a divine gift to which we owe awe and obedience. He has spoken often during his pontificate of the need to retrieve the ancient practice of *lectio divina*, the loving contemplation of Scripture in which reading is transformed into prayer.[75] And it is clear that he wants to move theology toward a more-prayerful and contemplative approach that is more like an intimate dialogue with the Lord who meets us and speaks to us in the sacred text. In addition to critical and scientific study, theology must include a "listening" in silence to the Word who comes to us not only in the Scriptures but also in the whole tradition of the Church.[76]

It is important to stress again, however, that Benedict envisions this prayerful contemplation of the sacred page as going hand-in-hand with historical and literary exegesis. It is important that theology not lose its connection to faith by becoming too exclusively rational or scientific. "A theology which no longer draws its life-breath from faith ceases to be theology; it ends up as an array of more or less loosely connected disciplines. But where theology is practiced 'on bent knee,' as Hans Urs von Balthasar urged, it will prove fruitful for the Church."[77] A theology on bended knee is a theology in service to the Word of God, following the witness of the New Testament authors, who lent their human "voices" to God that he might speak through them.

The theologian does not operate under any delusions of divine inspiration, yet he too seeks to be a faithful servant, making God's Word heard.

> The beautiful vocation of the theologian . . . means making present the Word, the Word who comes from God, the Word who is God. . . . God, in reality, is not the object but the subject of theology. The one who speaks through theology, the speaking subject, must be God himself. And our speech and thoughts must always serve to ensure that what God says, the Word of God, is listened to and

75. Pope Benedict XVI, Reflection on the Opening of the Eleventh Ordinary General Assembly of the Synod of Bishops (October 3, 2005), in *L'Osservatore Romano*, Weekly Edition in English (October 12, 2005), 7.

76. Pope Benedict XVI, Address to a Delegation of the Theological Faculty of the University of Tübingen (March 21, 2007).

77. Address, Visit to Heiligenkreuz Abbey (September 9, 2007).

finds room in the world. Thus once again we find ourselves invited to this process of forfeiting our own words, this process of purification so that our words may be nothing but the instrument through which God can speak, and hence, that he may truly be the subject and not the object of theology.[78]

Benedict's own Christian theology, and how it participates in the logic of God's self-revelation in the Church, will occupy us for the remainder of this essay. In this discussion, we will see the implications and the full development of the hermeneutical principles and methods that Benedict draws from as he takes the authors of Scripture as the "normative" theologians.

78. Pope Benedict XVI, Homily, Eucharistic Concelebration with the Members of the International Theological Commission (October 6, 2006).

5

Reading God's Testament
to Humankind

*Biblical Realism, Typology, and the Inner Unity
of Revelation*

A Biblical Character and the Stamp of the Fathers

We are almost in a position to sketch the fundamental outlines of
Benedict's biblical theology. The details of what I mean by "biblical
theology" should become clear during the course of the following discussion. In summary, biblical theology refers to a unified
understanding of the saving truths of the inspired Scripture as
they have been handed down in the tradition of the Church. This
understanding is based on the unity of the Old and New Testaments, on Christ as the interpretive key of the Scriptures, and on
the Church's divine liturgy as the fulfillment and actualization of
Scripture's saving truths. I have sought to ground Benedict's work
in his search for a new synthesis in theology, a synthesis that unites
the truths and imperatives of the faith with the tools of modern
historical and literary study of Scripture.

We first examined Benedict's critique of the historical-critical method, the method that today is held up in the academy and many seminaries as the best, most "scientific" way to read and understand the Bible. But in Benedict's critique, this method is shown to be constrained by its very nature as a "historical" discipline, which limits it to rendering hypotheses about the history of the biblical texts. It remains unable to fully help us understand the meaning of these texts for the Church today. Moreover, as Benedict shows, the method as it has developed is hampered by an underlying philosophy that erects a dialectic between faith and reason, presumes "discontinuity" between Scripture and the Church, and excludes from consideration all divine or supernatural referents in the biblical text.

We also examined Benedict's attempt to recover the form of the primitive Church and his belief that this original form should provide normative principles for the authentic growth and development of theology in continuity with the Church's tradition. His discovery of a deep unity and dialogic relation between the divine Word and the Church culminates in two significant assertions of methodological principle. First, a hermeneutic of faith offers us the greatest explanatory power of the biblical texts. Second, the authors of sacred Scripture should be regarded as normative for our approach to theology.

We need once again to stress that Benedict does not attempt to give us anything like a systematic theology. As he has said in autobiographical remarks:

> I have never tried to create a system of my own, an individual theology. . . . I simply want to think in communion with the faith of the Church, and that means above all to think in communion with the great thinkers of the faith. For this reason exegesis was always very important. I couldn't imagine a purely philosophical theology. The point of departure is first of all the Word. That we believe the Word of God, that we try really to get to know and understand it, and then, as I said, to think it together with the great masters of the faith. This gives my theology a somewhat biblical character and also bears the stamp of the Fathers, especially Augustine. But it goes without saying that I try not to stop with the ancient Church

but to hold fast to the great high points of thought and at the same
time to bring contemporary thought into the discussion.[1]

As we will see, this is an accurate appraisal of his work. Benedict's theology indeed bears a "biblical character" and reflects
the biblical, philosophical, and liturgical worldview that we find
in the Fathers of the Church. As we will also see, another defin-
ing characteristic of his work is his concern for prayer, worship,
and the liturgy. In a short reflection explaining why he wanted the
first volume of his *Opera Omnia* to be his collected writings on
liturgy, he said:

> Ever since my childhood, the Church's liturgy has been the central
> activity of my life, and it also became, under the theological in-
> struction of masters like [Michael] Schmaus, [Gottlieb] Söhngen,
> [Joseph] Pascher, and [Romano] Guardini, the center of my theo-
> logical work. I chose fundamental theology as my specific topic,
> because I wanted above all to go to the heart of the question: why
> do we believe? But right from the beginning, this question included
> the other one about the proper response to God, and therefore
> also the question about the divine service. It is on this basis that
> my work on the liturgy must be understood. I was not interested
> in the specific problems of liturgical study, but in the anchoring of
> the liturgy in the fundamental act of our faith, and therefore also
> its place in our entire human existence.[2]

Benedict is adamant that a hermeneutic of faith is not simply an
uncritical clinging to the literal words of Scripture or the patterns
of interpretation practiced in the early Church. Such a reading
would banish Christ to the distant past and render the faith ster-
ile.[3] Instead, he asserts that "unity is a fundamental principle of
theology, and we must learn to read . . . according to a hermeneutics

---

1. Joseph Cardinal Ratzinger with Peter Seewald, *Salt of the Earth: Christianity
and the Catholic Church at the End of the Millennium*, trans. Adrian Walker (San
Francisco: Ignatius, 1997), 66.
2. English translation published in Sandro Magister, "In the 'Opera Omnia' of
Ratzinger the Theologian, the Overture Is All about the Liturgy," available at http://
chiesa.espresso.repubblica.it/articolo/208933?eng=y.
3. *Ecumenism*, 7.

of unity, which shows up much that is new and opens doors where only bolts were visible before."[4]

In the same way, he insists that taking the Church's Fathers and liturgical and creedal traditions as normative is not a retreat into the misty past. "Normativity, when properly understood, does not mean the exclusion of the new, but guidance which points one toward what lies on the horizon. Striding forth into new country is made possible here precisely by the fact that the right path has been found."[5] At the same time, his theology also shows him to be in dialogue not only with Scripture and the Fathers and other elements of the great tradition but also with secular writers, composers, artists, scientists, and philosophers.

Benedict's theological project is undergirded by his departure point in the Word and his commitment to thinking in communion with the Church, that is, "within the synchronic and diachronic understanding of the faith."[6] By this he means that his theology seeks the meaning of the divine Word not in historical isolation or as if it were locked in the past but as that meaning has developed over time in the living subject of the Church. There is a great need today, he has said, for "diachronic *koinonia*—communion with the Church in every age."[7]

What Benedict has observed about the approach to theology in the thirteenth century is equally true for his approach: "it was clear that theology must not and could not be anything else but interpretation of Scripture."[8] In commenting about his own method, he always stresses the importance of biblical interpretation, going so far as to say: "Exegesis has always remained for me *the center* of my theological work."[9] It is important to keep in mind, however,

4. *Ecumenism*, 82: "Genuine identity with the origin is only to be found where there is also the living continuity that develops in and thus preserves it."
5. *Song*, 136.
6. *Way*, 152.
7. Pope Benedict XVI, Address to Ecumenical Prayer Service, St. Joseph's Parish, New York (April 18, 2008).
8. Joseph Ratzinger, "Sources and Transmission of the Faith," *Communio* 10, no. 1 (1983): 27.
9. Joseph Cardinal Ratzinger, *Milestones: Memoirs, 1927–1977*, trans. Erasmo Leiva-Merkiakis (San Francisco: Ignatius, 1998), 52–53; emphasis added. See also

that revelation for Benedict is not limited to the written word of Scripture.[10]

Faith Gives Us the Right to Trust the Revealed Word

We have already established Benedict's respect for and his use of the modern tools of exegesis. And, as we have also said, these tools of scientific reason are essential for him because the Scriptures not only speak of ideas or literary images but also make claims about the truths of history and the material world. Benedict's use of these methods is always guided by his hermeneutic of faith. The task, as he puts it, is "how to join its [the historical-critical method's] tools with a better philosophy, which would entail fewer drawbacks foreign to the text, which would be less arbitrary, and which would offer greater possibilities for a true listening to the text itself."[11]

Benedict rejects out of hand any historical or scientific approaches that would limit what we know by reason to sensory or experimental knowledge only. He offers this counsel to the exegete:

> Preparation is required to open us up to the inner dynamism of the Word. This is possible only when there is a certain sym-*pathia*, or understanding, a readiness to learn something new, to allow oneself to be taken along a new road. . . .

his Address to the Community of the Roman Major Seminary (February 17, 2007); *Theology*, 93. Benedict's views are mirrored in the Congregation for the Doctrine of the Faith's *Instruction on the Ecclesial Vocation of the Theologian*, which was issued under his signature as prefect of the Congregation: "[The theologian's] role is to pursue in a particular way an ever deeper understanding of the Word of God in the inspired Scriptures and handed on in the living tradition of the Church. . . . The object of theology is the truth which is the living God and his plan for salvation revealed in Jesus Christ" (in *L'Osservatore Romano*, Weekly Edition in English [July 2, 1990], 1).

10. Commenting on the Second Vatican Council's document *Dei Verbum*, he aligns himself with the Council's understanding of "Revelation, which is not to be wholly identified with its written testimony that is the Bible, and thus opens the vast historical and theological prospect in which biblical interpretation takes place, an interpretation that sees in the Scriptures not only human books but the testimony of divine speech" ("Magisterium").

11. "Interpretation," 254.

Thus the exegete should not approach the text with a ready-made philosophy, nor in accordance with the dictates of a so-called modern or scientific worldview, which determines in advance what may or may not be. He may not exclude a priori that (almighty) God could speak in human words in the world. He may not exclude that God himself could enter into and work in human history, however improbable such a thing might at first appear. He must be ready to learn from the extraordinary. He must be ready to accept that the truly original may occur in history, something which cannot be derived from precedents but which opens up out of itself. He may not deny to humanity the ability to be responsive beyond the categories of pure reason and to reach beyond ourselves toward the open and endless truth of being.[12]

The opinion that faith as such knows absolutely nothing of historical facts and must leave all of this to historians is gnosticism: this opinion disembodies faith and reduces it to pure idea. The reality of events is necessary precisely because the faith is founded on the Bible. *A God who cannot intervene in history and reveal himself in it is not the God of the Bible.* In this way the reality of the birth of Jesus by the Virgin Mary, the effective institution of the Eucharist by Jesus at the Last Supper, his bodily resurrection from the dead—this is the meaning of the empty tomb—are elements of the faith as such, which it can and must defend against an only presumably superior historical knowledge. That Jesus—in all that is essential—was effectively who the Gospels reveal him to be to us is not mere historical conjecture, but *a fact of faith.* Objections which seek to convince us to the contrary are not the expression of an effective scientific knowledge, but are an arbitrary over-evaluation of the method.[13]

Here we see Benedict's rehabilitation of reason in the exegetical process. The Christian faith is not faith in a series of propositions but faith in a historical person. Scripture is the historical record of the words and events associated with that person, who claims to represent the summation of a long historical process of God's dealings with humanity. Hence the theologian working with a

12. "Interpretation," 19.
13. "Magisterium"; emphasis added.

hermeneutic of faith must presume the historical "reality" or "facticity" of the words and events recorded in the text. Faith makes this presumption not only possible but also fruitful, enabling us to read in continuity with the living subject of the Church.

Of course, exegesis can and must also investigate the internal history of the texts in order to trace their development and thought patterns. We all know that there is much to learn from such work. But it must not lead us to neglect the principal task, which is to understand the text as it now stands, as a totality in itself with its own particular message. *Whoever reads Scripture in faith as a Bible must make a further step. . . . Faith makes us Jesus' contemporaries.* It can and must integrate all true historical discoveries, and it becomes richer for doing so. *But faith gives us knowledge of something more than a hypothesis; it gives us the right to trust the revealed Word as such.*[14]

This trust in the revealed Word is foundational for Benedict. What he says about the "biblical realism" of the *Catechism of the Catholic Church*, which he was instrumental in conceiving and editing, is no less true of his own theological thought: "The *Catechism* trusts the biblical word. It holds the Christ of the Gospels to be the real Jesus. It is also convinced that all the Gospels tell us about this same Jesus and that all of them together help us, each in its own way, to know the true Jesus of history, who is no other than the Christ of faith."[15]

For Benedict, "the biblical books . . . are, precisely, historical books."[16] This is the basic assumption of all his work, especially his work in Christology. In *Jesus of Nazareth* he accepts the historical reliability not only of the Synoptic Gospels—Matthew, Mark, and Luke—but also of John, which he suggests originates with an "eyewitness."[17] He accepts the Gospel testimony concerning Jesus

14. *Catechism*, 67–68; emphasis added.
15. *Catechism*, 64; see also 60–61: "An honest reader must admit without cavil that the [Catechism] is shaped from one end to the other by the Bible. As far as I know, there has never been until now a catechism so thoroughly formed by the Bible."
16. "Magisterium."
17. *Jesus*, 11, 227.

as factually correct, as an accurate reflection of Jesus' teaching, and as "a written record of the most ancient catechesis."[18] He has stated that on simply historical grounds, the testimony of the New Testament is far more trustworthy than the constantly shifting hypotheses of historical-critical scholarship.[19] "The history of exegesis is a history of contradictions; the daring constructions of many modern exegetes, right up to the materialistic interpretation of the Bible, show that the Word, if left alone as a book, is a helpless prey to manipulation through preexisting desires and opinions."[20] He challenges a seldom-questioned principle of the scholarly consensus among historical-critical exegetes, namely, that what eventually became Christian orthodoxy emerged only after a long process of debate among different communities with very different ideas and traditions concerning Jesus.

I believe that this Jesus—the Jesus of the Gospels—is a historically plausible and convincing figure. Unless there had been something extraordinary in what happened, unless the person and words of Jesus radically surpassed the hopes and expectations of the time, there is no way to explain why he was crucified or why he made such an impact. As early as twenty or so years after Jesus' death, the great Christ-hymn of the Letter to the Philippians (cf. Phil. 2:6–11) offers us a fully developed christology stating that Jesus was equal

18. *Catechism*, 61.
19. See *Dogma*, 9–10: "I credit biblical tradition with greater truthfulness than I do the attempts to reconstruct a chemically pure historical Jesus in the retort of historical reason. I trust the tradition in its entirety. And the more reconstructions I see come and go, the more I feel confirmed in my trust. It becomes increasingly clear to me that the interpretation given by Chalcedon is the only one that does not have to interpret anything away but is able to include everything. Any other interpretation must eliminate larger or smaller parts of the historical data in the name of its supposedly superior rational insights. But the authority that compels such decisions is only the authority of a particular way of thinking whose historical limitations can often be clearly shown. In the face of such partial authorities the vital power of the tradition carries incomparably greater weight with me. For this reason, I do not regard the dispute about the *ipsissima vox*, or actual words Jesus spoke, as very important. I know that the Jesus of the Gospels is the real Jesus and that I can trust myself to him with far greater security than I can to the most learned reconstructions; he will outlast all of them. The Gospel tradition with its great breadth and its range of tone tells me who Jesus was and is. In it he is always present to be heard and seen anew."
20. *Pilgrim*, 34.

to God, but emptied himself, became man, and humbled himself to die on the Cross, and that to him now belongs the worship of all creation, the adoration that God, through the prophet Isaiah, said was due to him alone (cf. Isa. 45:23).

Critical scholarship rightly asks the question: What happened during those twenty years after Jesus' crucifixion? Where did this christology come from? To say that it is the fruit of anonymous collective formulations, whose authorship we seek to discover, does not actually explain anything. How could these unknown groups be so creative? How were they so persuasive and how did they manage to prevail? Isn't it more logical, even historically speaking, to assume that the greatness came at the beginning, and that the figure of Jesus really did explode all existing categories and could only be understood in light of the mystery of God? Admittedly, to believe that, as man, he truly *was* God, and that he communicated his divinity veiled in parables, yet with increasing clarity, exceeds the scope of the historical method. Yet if instead we take this conviction of faith as our starting point for reading the texts with the help of historical methodology and its intrinsic openness to something greater, they are opened up and reveal a way and a figure that are worthy of belief. Something else comes into clear focus as well: Though the New Testament writings display a many-layered struggle to come to grips with the figure of Jesus, they exhibit a deep harmony despite all their difference.[21]

As Benedict presumes "the historical nature of Christianity as based on events,"[22] he also treats the Old Testament witness seriously as rooted in historical events.[23] The biblical record is a human history and a divine history. It is a human history shaped by its encounter with the living God. The succession of events in

---

21. *Jesus*, xxii–xxiii. See also *Jesus*, 303–4; *Catechism*, 66.

22. *Truth*, 89.

23. For example, he writes of "the whole history recounted in the books of the Judges and Kings, which is taken up afresh and given a new interpretation in Chronicles," and he uses the account of Israel's Exodus and settlement of the land as an insight into the meaning of worship (see *Liturgy*, 15–20). Likewise, he considers the history of liturgy from Genesis to the Christian era (*Liturgy*, 35–45) and discusses the biblical nature of wisdom in light of Isaiah's prophecy and the Davidic monarchy (*Principles*, 356–58). See also his discussion of Adam and Eve in "Message for the 80th World Mission Sunday 2006," *L'Osservatore Romano*, Weekly Edition in English (June 14, 2006), 3.

this history is unified by the Church, which joined the Old and New Testaments into one canonical text.

The Unity of Scripture and the Christological Hermeneutic

The unity of the Bible—the copenetration of the Old and New Testaments and their interpretation in the light of Christ—is a key to Benedict's biblical theology.[24] Here we see an important consequence of the hermeneutic of faith. It is the faith of the Church alone that makes the disparate texts into a single book, into a Bible. "Without faith, Scripture itself is not Scripture, but rather an ill-assorted ensemble of bits of literature that cannot claim any normative significance."[25] In fact, this inability to discern the unity of Scripture, which is a consequence of the historical-critical method presuming that a discontinuity lies between the Church and the Word, is one of the key problems with this method as it is currently practiced.

Alternately, by faith the theologian not only can trust the basic reliability of the historical texts but also is able to see the internal unity of Scripture, the connections and patterns that exist within and between texts.[26] A unified way of reading the Scriptures is

24. Benedict writes approvingly of the Second Vatican Council's "understanding of Holy Scripture as an inner unity in which one part sustains the other, has its existence in it, so that each part can be read and understood only in terms of the whole" (*Principles*, 135–36).

25. *Benedict XVI*, 146. "Since the inner unity of the books of the New Testament, and that of the two Testaments, can only be seen in the light of faith's interpretation, where this is lacking, people are forever separating out new components and discovering contradictions in the sources. Then, as a result, the figure of Jesus also is continually splitting into new pictures of Jesus: there is the Jesus of the logia, the Jesus of this or that community, Jesus the philanthropist, Jesus the Jewish rabbi, the apocalyptic Jesus, Jesus the Zealot, Jesus the revolutionary, the political Jesus, etc. In all these cases some preconceived idea determines the principles of interpretation; once these have been adopted, the historical method is applied, with varying degrees of care and subtlety, in order to try to prove, to oneself and to others, that the Jesus of one's own preconceptions is the only possible historical Jesus. In reality this process of dividing-up only reflects the divisions in man's mind and in the world; indeed, the process only serves to intensify them" (*Pierced*, 44). See also Pope Benedict XVI, Homily, Chrism Mass of Holy Thursday (April 13, 2006).

26. Benedict aligns himself, generally speaking, with the movement of "canonical exegesis" (see *Catechism*, 67). "'Canonical exegesis'—reading the individual texts of the Bible in the context of the whole—is an essential dimension of exegesis. It does

rooted, as we suggested in the last chapter, in the preaching of Jesus, who "imparted his message as a new interpretation of the Old Testament" and thereby made this way of reading normative for the New Testament writers.[27] To make this point, Benedict frequently returns to the almost programmatic description in the Gospel of Luke of the post-Easter Jesus teaching his disciples that the prophets, psalms, and the books of Moses—the entire Old Testament—are to be read in reference to his coming.[28]

This, as we saw earlier, is what Benedict calls the "christological hermeneutic."[29] This hermeneutic views Christ as the hinge, the unity of the Scriptures, the "one that Moses and the prophets had spoken of," and thus as the principle uniting and explaining the Old and New Testaments.[30] Read as a whole with a hermeneutic of faith, Scripture is seen as having its own dynamic that moves inexorably toward the figure of Christ.[31] "The New Testament itself wished to be no more than the complete and full understanding of the Old Testament, now made possible in Christ. The whole Old Testament is a movement of transition to Christ, a waiting for the One in whom all its words would come true, in whom the 'covenant' would attain fulfillment as the new covenant."[32]

Benedict's work is always informed by a deep knowledge and generous appreciation of Jewish history, traditions, and ritual. This can be seen most clearly in his remarkable and lengthy engagement in *Jesus of Nazareth* with the scholarship of Rabbi Jacob Neusner.[33] It is beyond the constraints of the present essay to discuss Benedict's understanding of the mystery of God's covenant relationship

---

not contradict historical-critical interpretation, but carries it forward in an organic way toward becoming theology in the proper sense" (*Jesus*, xviii–xix).

27. *Pilgrim*, 146.

28. See Luke 24:27, 44–45.

29. *Jesus*, xix.

30. *Catechism*, 52n17, 53.

31. See *Song*, 72: "The synthesis of the testaments worked out in the early Church corresponds solely to the fundamental intention of the New Testament message, and it alone can give Christianity its own historical force."

32. *Faith*, 58. See also *Jesus*, 56.

33. See *Jesus*, 102–22, which is an extended meditation on Rabbi Neusner's *A Rabbi Talks with Jesus: An Intermillennial, Interfaith Exchange* (New York: Doubleday, 1993).

with the Jewish people. He has quoted the beautiful words of his predecessor, Pope Pius XI, who said of Christians, "Spiritually, we are Semites." By this Benedict understands that "the Church herself is situated within the eternal covenant of the Almighty, whose plans are immutable, and she respects the children of the promise, the children of the covenant, as her beloved brothers and sisters in the faith."[34] Benedict sees the Almighty's covenant plan as singular and as oriented toward the inclusion of all humanity: "Right from the beginning, the promise to Abraham guarantees salvation history's inner continuity from the patriarchs of Israel down to Christ and to the Church of Jews and Gentiles."[35]

What is important for us is to recognize that Benedict's theology and exegesis presume as absolutely vital the unity of salvation history—reflected in the unity of the Old and New Testaments—and the principle that Jesus Christ is both the culmination of that history and the interpretative key of God's revelation in the Scriptures.

The Transcendent Meaning of Biblical Words

The unity of Scripture's covenant structure, which we will explore more fully below, suggests that the meaning of the biblical text

34. Pope Benedict XVI, Address to Representatives of the Jewish Community (September 12, 2008).

35. *Religions*, 68. See also Benedict's Message to the Jewish Community on the Feast of *Pesah* (April 14, 2008): "With the passing of time the Covenant assumes an ever more universal value, as the promise made to Abraham takes form: 'I will bless you and make your name great, so that you will be a blessing. . . . All the communities of the earth shall find blessing in you' (Gen. 12:2–3). Indeed, according to the prophet Isaiah, the hope of redemption extends to the whole of humanity: 'Many peoples will come and say: "Come, let us go up to the mountain of the Lord, to the house of the God of Jacob; that he may teach us his ways and that we may walk in his paths"' (Isa. 2:3). Within this eschatological horizon is offered a real prospect of universal brotherhood on the path of justice and peace, preparing the way of the Lord (compare Isa. 62:10). Christians and Jews share this hope; we are in fact, as the prophets say, 'prisoners of hope' (Zech. 9:12). This bond permits us Christians to celebrate alongside you, though in our own way, the Passover of Christ's death and resurrection, which we see as inseparable from your own, for Jesus himself said: 'salvation is from the Jews' (John 4:22). Our Easter and your *Pesah*, while distinct and different, unite us in our common hope centered on God and his mercy. They urge us to cooperate with each other and with all men and women of goodwill to make this a better world for all as we await the fulfillment of God's promises."

exists on at least two levels: the literal and historical and the "spiritual." The latter refers to the meaning of the text that can only be gained by faith in the claims made about God in these texts.

This twofold meaning is not imposed on the text as the result of some philosophical presupposition or methodological principle. Rather, it emerges from the structure of biblical revelation. The Bible, in its final canonical form, purports to document historical events, first events in the life of Israel and later events in the life of Christ and his Church. But these events are more than moments in the lives of a people. The Bible claims that God himself was at work in the events it records and that the words of various characters and their deeds represent the active intention of God.[36]

This consideration of the structure of biblical history informs Benedict's particular contribution to the Church's understanding of both the inspiration and the "senses" of Scripture. He builds his understandings on the findings of source criticism, which have shown how the various texts were shaped and formed through constant rereadings and reinterpretations over centuries.[37] This process highlights the decisive nature of the Church as the living subject of the Word. "Inspiration," then, is part of the dialogic dynamic inherent in the relation between the Word of God and the people of God who receive this Word, interpret it, and hand it on.

Because they are borne in the Church, which is the living subject of the Word, the meanings of scriptural texts cannot be "fixed to a particular moment in history."[38] Instead, as scholars have learned from studying the history of the texts and the process of their composition, later Scriptures are always in dialogue with earlier ones, commenting on and reinterpreting them.

> The Word of the Bible . . . was not frozen at the moment it was written down, but entered into new processes of interpretation— "relectures"—that further develop its hidden potential. Thus, the extent of the Word's meaning cannot be reduced to the thoughts of a single author in a specific historical moment; it is not the property

36. *Way*, 147–48.
37. *Pilgrim*, 32; *Jesus*, xviii.
38. "Preface," 17.

of a single author at all; rather, it lives in a history that is ever moving onward and, thus, has dimensions and depths of meaning in past and future that ultimately pass into the realm of the unforeseen. It is only at this point that we can begin to understand the nature of inspiration; we can see where God mysteriously enters into what is human and purely human authorship is transcended.[39]

This understanding of inspiration has two important implications for Benedict's reading and interpreting of the sacred texts. First, it leads to the methodological assumption that the literal word of the biblical text always contains greater depths, or a "surplus,"[40] of meaning. It will always mean more than it literally says. In part, this is also true of any human word that is spoken with any kind of significance. Such words by their nature will communicate "more than the author may have been immediately aware at the time."[41]

Benedict attributes this to the "multidimensional nature of human language,"[42] in which what is said contains deeper values that are left unsaid. What is true of human speech is even more true of the speech of God. "If even human speech boundlessly transcends itself the greater it is and refers to the unsaid and inexhaustible beyond the words themselves, how much more must this be true of the Word whose ultimate and real subject we believe to be God himself?"[43]

As the words of Scripture, by their very nature, must admit of more than their literal meaning, the same is true of the historical events recorded in Scripture. This insight, too, naturally follows from the structure of biblical revelation, that is, from the fact that "the Spirit is active, who guides actions and events in the Word and, in the events and actions, propels back to the Word."[44] Thus while the events recorded in the Bible are factual, their meanings far transcend "historical facticity" because God in his Spirit is their author. Indeed, because God is acting in the biblical narrative, "*the events carry within themselves a surplus meaning* . . . giving

39. *Pilgrim*, 32–33.
40. *Pilgrim*, 32.
41. *Jesus*, xix.
42. "Preface," 17.
43. *Song*, 50–51. See also *Benedict XVI*, 351.
44. *Way*, 148–49.

them significance for all time and for all men."[45] As Benedict said above, God, through the Spirit of inspiration, is active, guiding the events and actions recorded in Scripture. The divine meaning of scriptural events is not the product of some arbitrary rereading of the events after the fact. The meaning of the events recorded in the biblical text is contained *within* the original events. It is "present in the event, even though it transcends mere facticity."[46] For example, as we will consider in detail in the next chapter, Benedict believes that the Passover liturgy of the Jews was oriented toward its fulfillment in the Eucharist of Jesus. The institution of the Eucharist by Jesus at the Last Supper, then, is part of the "surplus" of meaning intended in the biblical event of the Passover. Benedict can even say: "Jesus introduced his words at the Last Supper organically into the Jewish liturgy at the point where it was open to them, as it were, *waiting for them.*"[47]

For the theologian, this means that it is not enough to seek the literal meaning of the text, that is, the surface meaning of what was said or what actually happened at the time of the text's composition. Understanding the literal meaning, even in terms of the sources, forms, and contexts, does not exhaust the meaning of the text. The theologian and exegete must also seek to understand the meaning that God intended in these words and events. Hence Benedict says we must read the sacred page in such a way as to hear "the living Speaker himself." We must "once again develop methods that respect this inner self-transcending of the words into the Word of God."[48] Practically speaking, this means accepting in faith the implications of what modern historical criticism has shown to us.

The fundamental and all-important hermeneutical insight here is that subsequent history belongs intrinsically to the inner momen-

---

45. *Way*, 148.
46. See the discussion in *Way*, 147–48.
47. *Faith*, 67; emphasis added.
48. *Song*, 50–51. We must also be vigilant in seeking "a greater understanding of how the Word of God can avail of the human word to confer on a history in progress a meaning that surpasses the present moment and yet brings out, precisely in this way, the unity of the whole" ("Preface," 17). See also *Eschatology*, 42–44.

tum of the text itself. That is: it does not simply provide retrospective commentary on the text. Rather, through the appearing of the reality which was still to come, the full dimensions of the Word carried by the text come to light. For this reason, the interpretation of these texts must be, by its very nature, incomplete. For this reason also, a generation later, John could penetrate in authoritative fashion the depth of the Word, and understand what was meant by it with greater purity than could his predecessors. For this reason, once again, his message is not simply a subsequent adaptation of the Word to a changed situation, but reproduces the inner movement of the Word itself. For this reason, finally, that kind of reconstruction which confines itself to the text in its earliest form and permits interpretation only on that basis is fundamentally out of order. . . . Only through the harvest of historical experience does the Word gradually gain its full meaning. . . .

And so the history of the Church continues in a certain respect what happened by way of foundation in the time of Jesus. . . . The words of the Old Testament, in which Israel's faith-experience of the Word of God is reflected, anticipate the history of Jesus, the living Word of God in this world. It is only in the light of that earlier Word that the figure of Jesus becomes theologically intelligible. Jesus is interpreted on its basis, and only thus can his whole existence be acknowledged as substantially "Word." And yet, no matter to what degree the biblical Word interpreted him ahead of time, only the real figure of him-who-came makes visible what remained hidden within the linguistic word alone and resisted extraction by purely historical means. The tension between old Word and new reality remains the fundamental form of Christian faith. Only by means of it can the hidden reality of God become known.[49]

Typology and the Symphony of the Testaments

The human word of Scripture contains within itself an openness to what lies beyond, to the transcendent, divine Word that inspires it. This means that the words *and the events* of Scripture are oriented toward their final fulfillment. Benedict's own work has assimilated the traditional Catholic concept of the four senses of Scripture—

49. *Eschatology*, 42–44.

the literal, historical sense, together with the allegorical, moral, and anagogical senses—which he has called "the four degrees of exegesis."[50] He is well aware that the latter three senses, sometimes referred to collectively as composing the "spiritual sense," have largely been discarded and discredited as unhistorical and arbitrary by scientific biblical interpreters. For him this is another symptom of how modern scholarship has lost sight of the unity of Scripture.

Benedict's analysis, however, suggests that the scholarly rejection of this traditional understanding of the texts is itself unhistorical and arbitrary. The spiritual sense of Scripture is what keeps the text from fragmenting and fading into a heap of dead letters that bear witness only to a primitive reality. Moreover, as we have seen, the spiritual sense—the orientation toward what fulfills and transcends the words and events—is inherent in the biblical text, which speaks not only of human events but also of the action of God in those events.

The basic error of historical criticism here is the decoupling of Word and event. Modern exegetes regard the events spoken of in Scripture, paradoxically, as either accidental or necessary. This means that according to their idea of the scientific method, events are either "accidents" that have occurred in nature or they are "necessary" outcomes resulting from prior events or occurrences. In either case, the events themselves have no intrinsic "meaning." They cannot be regarded as bearing any meaning apart from their relationship to other events or occurrences in nature. Thus when the modern exegete speaks of biblical events, he or she cannot regard them as bearing any divine meaning. At best, the events recorded in Scripture are examples or illustrations of what God wants to communicate, but the events themselves are only brute or mere facts.

This position follows from historical criticism's assumption that only what can be verified according to the experimental criteria of the natural sciences is valid subject matter for interpretation. Since the events recounted in the Bible cannot be demonstrated in this manner, they are left aside as having no "knowable" meaning for the interpreter.

50. Ratzinger, "Sources," 29.

Here we have another instance of the incompatibility of historical criticism's underlying scientific philosophy and the unique challenges of biblical interpretation. "What is useful as a methodological principle for the natural sciences is a foregone banality as a philosophical principle; and as a theological principle it is a contradiction. (How can any or all of God's activity be considered either accidental or necessary?)"[51] Such a dualism of biblical Word and event only reinforces the artificial discontinuities historical critics see in the text. The "events" of the New Testament are made to have no ascertainable reference to the "events" of the Old because the "activity" of Christ is understood not as historical but as only apparent.

Only the spiritual understanding of Scripture, which recognizes how the historical word is open to the transcendent dimensions of divine action, helps us to penetrate the meaning of Scripture.

> Certainly texts must first of all be traced back to their historical origins and interpreted in their proper historical context. But then, in a second exegetical operation, one must look at them also in light of the total movements of history and history's central event, Jesus Christ. Only the *combination of both* of these methods will yield a correct understanding of the Bible.[52]

Again we see the close relationship between faith and reason in Benedict's method. We also see that the essence of the "spiritual sense" lies in the *typological* reading of Scripture, a reading that sees the unity of God's actions in history and understands the long unfolding of Israel's history as pointing toward and culminating in Jesus Christ. In this typological reading, historical events and the divine Word are united in the singular action and intention of God.

Typology, as the essence of the spiritual sense of Scripture, reveals the unity and coherence of history in light of that "central event" of history, the coming of the Word of God in the flesh.[53]

51. "Interpretation," 255.
52. "Interpretation," 256; emphasis added.
53. For Benedict, the meaning of Scripture is a "meaning in which the human word and God's Word work together in the singularity of historical events and the eternity of the everlasting Word which is contemporary in every age. The biblical Word comes

For Benedict, then, the multiple "senses" of Scripture are better understood as "the four dimensions of meaning in the text."[54] Noting the literary history of the texts in their "ongoing process of revision," Benedict says that recognition of the Church's traditional systematizing of scriptural senses is "scientifically appropriate given the nature of this unique structure of texts."[55] These dimensions open the text to the true and spiritual meaning of history, which is ordered by God and toward God.[56]

Benedict describes his own theological project as a synthesis by which he is attempting to unfold the spiritual meaning of the history recorded in the Scriptures.[57] And not only does he assert the insufficiency of modern exegesis's exclusive focus on the literal and historical word of Scripture, he also argues that unless we penetrate to the spiritual sense of Scripture we will never really understand it. Without understanding in the Spirit on our part, he says, there is no "revelation" in the scriptural text. "There can be Scripture without revelation. For revelation always and only becomes a reality where there is faith."[58]

He grounds his point in Paul's discussion of the old and new covenants in 2 Corinthians 3. For Benedict, the person who reads without the Spirit of Christ (2 Cor. 3:17) may comprehend the literary forms, the historical context, and the meaning of the Greek or

---

from a real past. It comes not only from the past, however, but at the same time from the eternity of God, and leads us into God's eternity, but again along the way through time, to which the past, the present, and the future belong" (Joseph Cardinal Ratzinger, "Preface," Pontifical Biblical Commission, *The Interpretation of the Bible in the Church*, in *The Scripture Documents: An Anthology of Official Catholic Teachings*, ed. Dean P. Béchard, SJ [Collegeville, MN: Liturgical Press, 2002], 245).

54. *Way*, 151.

55. *Way*, 150.

56. See *Catechism*, 65n24: "Spiritual [interpretation] does not mean that the exegesis lacks realism or disregards history but that it brings into view the spiritual depth of the historical events."

57. See Pope Benedict XVI, General Audience (April 25, 2007): "It is the Holy Spirit who enables us to understand the christological content, hence, the unity in diversity of Scripture. It would be interesting to demonstrate this. I have made a humble attempt in my book, *Jesus of Nazareth*, to show in today's context these multiple dimensions of the Word, of sacred Scripture, whose historical meaning must in the first place be respected."

58. "Revelation," 36.

Hebrew terms, but his or her knowledge will remain "veiled." The reader will not be able to access the "inner reality" of the text, which is disclosed only to those who read in the Spirit, that is, in the light of Christ.[59] In this, Benedict shows the influence of the patristic interpretive tradition and of St. Bonaventure's theology. "The true meaning of Scripture will be found only in reaching behind the letters," he says, making Bonaventure's teaching his own.[60]

Benedict's reading of Bonaventure highlights the dialogic structure of revelation and the importance of the ecclesial structure of the faith for interpretation. Spiritual interpretation is not private or subjective, meaning it is not determined by the caprice of the individual interpreter. The principle of spiritual exegesis is always found in the Church—in the rule of faith, in the *symbol*, and in the liturgy. Theology and exegesis become a matter not of the theologian's personal creativity but of his or her faithful endeavor to seek the meaning of the text in communion with the Church, the living subject of the Word. Revelation comes in this faithful reading from the heart of the Church, in which *sacra scriptura* becomes *theologia*.

> Only Scripture as it is understood in faith is truly holy Scripture. Consequently, Scripture in the full sense is theology, that is, it is the book *and* the understanding of the book in the faith of the Church. On the other hand, theology can be called Scripture, for it is nothing other than the understanding of Scripture; this understanding, which is theology, brings Scripture to that full fruitfulness which corresponds to its nature as Revelation. . . . The understanding which elevates the Scripture to the status of "Revelation" is not to be taken as an affair of the individual reader, but is realized only in the living understanding of Scripture in the Church. . . . In other words, such an understanding demands the attitude of faith by which man gains entrance into the living understanding of Scripture in the Church. It is in this way that man truly receives "Revelation."[61]

59. "Revelation," 36.
60. Joseph Ratzinger, *The Theology of History in St. Bonaventure*, trans. Zachary Hayes (Chicago: Franciscan Herald, 1971), 66–67.
61. Ratzinger, *St. Bonaventure*, 66–68, 77–78.

The importance of typology for Benedict's own theology is brought out in his series of general audience talks on the Fathers of the Church in 2007 and 2008. The theological project of the Fathers, as he presents it, is centered on the unity of the Bible. That unity, the Fathers' interpretive key to the Scriptures, was Jesus Christ himself.

The typological or christological interpretation of the Old Testament that begins in the New Testament continues in the Fathers. Christ solves the problem of how the Old Testament relates to the New, how the Gospel relates to the Law. The Old Testament is to be read as "a journey toward Jesus Christ."[62] Understood in the light of Christ, Israel's national history is transformed into a universal history that embraces all peoples. Benedict's vision is similar to what he finds in the writings of Cyril of Jerusalem—"a 'symphonic' relationship between the two Testaments, arriving at Christ, the center of the universe."[63]

On a practical level, these insights mean that Benedict always reads the New Testament in light of the Old and the Old Testament in light of the New. Individual passages in Scripture are "read and understood only in terms of the whole,"[64] and "the whole derives its meaning from its end—from Christ."[65] Benedict often quotes Augustine: "The New Testament lies hidden in the Old; the Old is made explicit in the New."[66]

In addition to this commitment to an exegesis that respects the content and unity of the Bible, Benedict also reads in faithful continuity with the Church's liturgical and dogmatic tradition.[67] The Church's conciliar creeds and the interpretations of the biblical legacy found in the Church's liturgical worship are almost equally authoritative for interpreting the text.[68] "The Church's

---

62. Pope Benedict XVI, General Audience (January 9, 2008).

63. Pope Benedict XVI, General Audience (June 27, 2007).

64. *Principles*, 135–36.

65. *Beginning*, 9.

66. *Religions*, 36.

67. Benedict's methods reflect the "criteria" found in the Catholic magisterial tradition. See *Dei Verbum* 12 and *Catechism of the Catholic Church*, nos. 112–14.

68. See *Liturgy*, 167: "Because of the historical character of God's action, the 'Divine Liturgy' (as they call it in the East) has been fashioned, in a way similar to Scripture,

liturgy being the original interpretation of the biblical heritage has no need to justify itself before historical reconstructions: it is rather itself the standard, sprung from what is living, which directs research back to the initial stages."[69] He notes that the Church's christological beliefs in particular were shaped by the liturgy[70] and that entire parts of the New Testament are in fact about liturgy and worship.[71]

> The liturgy is the true, living environment for the Bible. . . . The Bible can be properly understood only in this living context within which it first emerged. The texts of the Bible, this great book of Christ, are not to be seen as the literary products of some scribes at their desks, but rather as the words of Christ himself delivered in the celebration of holy Mass. *The scriptural texts are thoroughly imbued with the awe of divine worship* resulting from the believer's interior attentiveness to the living voice of the present Lord.[72]

The connections and interpretations among the texts found in the Church's liturgy have a normative authority for Benedict. This is due, in part, because the prayerful disposition of worship aids the believer in hearing more fully the living voice of Christ in the texts. The Word heard in the liturgy is heard in the "great communion of the Church of all times . . . in the great 'we' of the Church, where the Word of God is alive."[73] As we will see when we consider the Mass, the liturgy gives the biblical Word its fulfill-

---

by human beings and their capacities. But it contains an essential exposition of the biblical legacy that goes beyond the limits of individual rites, and thus it shares in the authority of the Church's faith in its fundamental form. *The authority of the liturgy can certainly be compared to that of the great confessions of faith of the early Church.* Like these, it developed under the guidance of the Holy Spirit (John 16:13)" (emphasis added).

69. *Ecumenism*, 84–85.

70. *Song*, 104.

71. *Liturgy*, 185–86.

72. Joseph Cardinal Ratzinger, introduction to *The Lord*, by Romano Guardini (Washington, DC: Regnery, 1996 [1954]), xii; emphasis added.

73. Pope Benedict XVI, Address to Lenten Meeting with the Clergy of Rome (February 22, 2007).

ment. "Interpretation becomes prayer and is united with Christ's prayer in the Eucharistic Prayer."[74] This focus on the liturgical or sacramental reading of Scripture once again highlights the importance of typology for Benedict. Particularly in the liturgies of Advent, Lent, and Easter, the Church "uses the typological exegesis of Scripture in order to situate us in a certain spiritual context and continuity."[75] And as we will see in the chapters to come, Benedict's biblical theology is itself ordered to the liturgical encounter with the living Word that speaks in Scripture, bringing about the very promises that it speaks of in the life of the believer. "Scripture alive in the living Church is also God's present power in the world today—a power which remains an inexhaustible source of hope throughout all generations."[76]

74. Address to the Community of the Roman Major Seminary (February 17, 2007).
75. *Dogma*, 29. Cf. *Catechism of the Catholic Church*, nos. 1094–95.
76. *Song*, 52.

6

The Theology of the Divine Economy

Covenant, Kingdom, and the History of Salvation

The Covenant as the Meaning of the Divine Economy

Because he reads Scripture typologically as a unity (and makes use of the insights afforded by modern historical and literary tools), the Bible tells a "coherent story" for Benedict.[1] It is the story of God's creation and salvation of the human race. For Benedict this typological reading, which consists in "the elucidation of signs" found in the biblical text, reveals a divine "economy" or salvation history.[2]

Although he apparently prefers to talk about "salvation history" rather than the divine "economy," Benedict's understanding of salvation history reflects the patristic distinction between economy (*oikonomia*) and theology (*theologia*), wherein the economy consists of the deeds and words by which God reveals himself in his-

1. *Way*, 147. See also *Benedict XVI*, 215.
2. *Principles*, 317; for Benedict's discussion of the theological issues of salvation and history, see *Principles*, 153–90.

tory, and theology refers to the inner trinitarian life of God that is revealed to us by the economy.[3]

Adopting another patristic term, Benedict sees in the economy the outworking of a divine "pedagogy." By a long historical tutelage that culminates in the revelation of Christ, God is adapting the human race to his own ways and preparing humans for communion with him. In saying this, Benedict embraces the ideas of St. Irenaeus.[4] The divine pedagogical intent is the meaning of the Old and New Testaments as understood in their "inner continuity and coherence."[5] In fact, as Benedict sees it, "The totality of the Scriptures on which the Christian faith rests is God's 'testament' to mankind, issued in two stages, as a proclamation of his will to the world."[6]

The divine economy, then, is the content of Scripture. This economy, by which the history of the Old and New Testaments is unified into a single history of salvation in Christ, reveals a theology, the "mind" or intention of God. God's intent, his will for the world, is his *testamentum*, or covenant, with humanity. By his covenant, God desires to father his people, making all men and women one family with him in a communion of love. The plan of the covenant, which Benedict calls an "ineffable plan of love,"[7] is the ultimate content and meaning of Scripture. This notion of covenant and economy in turn lies at the heart of Benedict's Christology and ecclesiology, which is expressed in his magisterial teaching that the Church is "God's family," the living subject by which "the Father . . . wishes to make humanity a single family in his Son."[8]

Benedict's biblical theology of the covenant synthesizes a great deal of scholarship, beginning with the modern exegetical finding

---

3. *Principles*, 172.
4. See *Catechism*, 32; *Religions*, 55–56; *Pilgrim*, 270; *Principles*, 344–45; *Beginning*, 9, 16. On Irenaeus, see Pope Benedict XVI, Homily, Solemnity of Ss. Peter and Paul (June 29, 2005).
5. *Religions*, 36.
6. *Religions*, 47.
7. Pope Benedict XVI, Homily, Mass in Blonie Park, Krakow (May 28, 2006).
8. Pope Benedict XVI, *Deus Caritas Est*, Encyclical Letter on Christian Love (December 25, 2005), 19, 25.

that "the internal beginning of the Old Testament lies . . . with the reality of the covenant."[9] He presents the covenant not as a contractual relationship entered into by parties of equal standing but as being "modeled after" ancient Near Eastern pacts between feudal lords and their vassals. "The 'covenant' is not a two-sided contract but a gift, a creative act of God's love. . . . God, the King, receives nothing from man; but in giving him his law, he gives him the path of life."[10]

As in other ancient Near Eastern cultures, the notion of covenant in the Hebrew Bible is ordered to kinship, that is, to the creation of a kind of "blood relationship" or filial bond between God and his people.[11] In the biblical covenant we see the true image of God and the true image of the human person. The covenant shows the human to be made for relationship with God, who is the "ground of his existence." At the same time the covenant reveals itself as *who God is*. In it we see the perfect "manifestation of his self, the 'radiance of his countenance.'"[12]

In Benedict's view, God's testament or covenant is "the central theme of Scripture itself, thus giving a key to the whole of it."[13] Covenant provides the narrative structure of Scripture, with the canonical text unfolding in the sequence of covenants that God makes: with Noah, with Abraham, with Moses and Israel, and finally with David. The plurality and interrelatedness of these covenants forms the single "old covenant," which points to its fulfillment in the new covenant made by Jesus Christ.[14]

9. "Problems in Catechesis Today: An Interview with Joseph Cardinal Ratzinger," *Communio* 11, no. 2 (1984): 151–52.

10. *Religions*, 50–51.

11. *Religions*, 60–61. See also Joseph Cardinal Ratzinger, "The New Covenant: A Theology of Covenant in the New Testament," *Communio* 22, no. 4 (1995): 635–51, esp. 636–37.

12. *Religions*, 77.

13. *Religions*, 48.

14. See *Religions*, 57: "The one covenant is realized in the plurality of covenants. If this is so, there can be no question of setting the Old and the New Testaments against each other as two different religions; there is only *one* will of God for men, only *one* historical activity of God with and for men, though this activity employs interventions that are diverse and even contradictory—yet in truth they belong together."

The Goal of Creation and the Soul of Worship

Benedict reads God's covenant will and desire beginning on the very first pages of Scripture in the account of creation. He does so through an exegesis that sees parallels in the canonical text between the creation of heaven and earth and Moses' building of the tabernacle. In both the Genesis and the Exodus accounts, a place is being made for God to dwell with his covenant people. There is also the centrality in each account of a rhythm involving the cosmically significant number seven and the law of the seventh day, the Sabbath, which is a law of worship.

The world, as Benedict sees it, is fashioned by God to be the sacred space in which his covenant can be established. "The goal of creation is the covenant, the love story of God and man."[15]

> Creation is oriented to the Sabbath, which is the sign of the covenant between God and humankind. . . . As a first step, we can draw this conclusion: Creation is designed in such a way that it is oriented to worship. It fulfills its purpose and assumes its significance when it is lived, ever new, with a view to worship. Creation exists for the sake of worship. As St. Benedict said in his Rule: *Operi Dei nihil praeponatur*—"Nothing must be put before the service of God." This is not the expression of an otherworldly piety but a clear and sober translation of the creation account and of the message that it bears for our lives. The true center, the power that moves and shapes from within in the rhythm of the stars and of our lives, is worship. . . . The universe exists for worship and for the glorification of God.[16]

We notice here another important characteristic of Benedict's theological work. The work of theology for him is never simply academic or for the sake of learning alone. It is always in the service of the Word. In this case, for instance, he does not limit himself to explaining the meaning of the biblical creation ac-

---

15. *Liturgy*, 26–27.

16. *Beginning*, 27–28. See also *Jesus*, 83: "The Sabbath is the goal of creation, and it shows what creation is for. The world exists, in other words, because God wanted to create a zone of response to his love, a zone of obedience and freedom."

count. He wants his readers to know the implications of this biblical text for their lives. This is a constant in Benedict's writing. It lends his biblical theology an urgency that is rare in scholarly theology today.

To return to our discussion of his project, the world was created to be a temple-kingdom of God. The human person, made "in the image of God," is given a priestly vocation, namely, to offer worship to God. In Benedict's writings, we see the importance of the dialogic or relational character of the human person. Man is created in and for relation and dialogue with God, who in turn is a communion of divine persons, a Trinity.[17] The call of the loving God addressed to the human person is a call to a relationship of love and communion. The human response takes the form of prayer, worship, and freely given obedience in love to the divine Word that is spoken.

Hence we see that for Benedict, "worship, law, and ethics are inseparably interwoven" in God's covenant relationship with man.[18] God's covenant Word is always expressed as law and liturgy. This is seen most clearly in the giving of the Law at Sinai, which includes the Sabbath ordinances as part of "a covenant concretized in a minutely regulated form of worship."[19] Throughout the Scriptures there is found a profound inner connection between the "legal and cultic" orders, between the moral order and the liturgical order,

17. Summarizing the development of the theological notion of personhood in the writings of the Fathers, Benedict writes: "The concept of 'person' grew out of reading the Bible, as something needed for its interpretation. It is a product of reading the Bible. Secondly, it grew out of the idea of dialogue, more specifically, it grew as an explanation of the phenomenon of the God who speaks dialogically. The Bible with its phenomenon of the God who speaks, the God who is *in* dialogue, stimulated the concept of 'person.' The particular interpretations of Scripture texts offered by the Fathers are certainly accidental and outdated. But their exegetical direction as a whole captures the spiritual direction of the Bible inasmuch as the fundamental phenomenon into which we are placed by the Bible is the God who speaks and the human person who is addressed, the phenomenon of the partnership of the human person who is called by God to love in the world" (Joseph Ratzinger, "Concerning the Notion of Person in Theology," *Communio* 17, no. 3 [1990]: 443). See also *Beginning*, 47–48; *Religions*, 75–77.

18. *Liturgy*, 18.

19. *Liturgy*, 17.

between the commands and ordinances of God and the sacrificial worship of God.[20]

Law and worship are two sides of the covenant relationship, which is intended by God as a relationship of filial love. The legal and cultic orders are "an expression of God's love, of his 'yes' to the human being that he created, so that he [the human being] could both love and receive love. . . . God created the universe in order to enter into a history of love with humankind. He created it so that love could exist."[21]

Worship is "the soul of the covenant." God's purposes for creation are realized through the worship offered by the human person created in his image and likeness. Human worship "not only saves mankind but is also meant to draw the whole of reality into communion with God."[22] For Benedict, our worship is meant to take the form of a giving back, a handing over of our selves and our possessions to God in an act of thanksgiving and love. Authentic worship never begins as human initiative but rather is always a response to the divine gift. In its purest form, worship is sacrifice; "the only real gift man should give to God is himself."[23]

God's purpose in this primal order of covenant worship is what Benedict calls *theiosis*, or divinization, a term he adopts from the Eastern Fathers of the Church.[24]

> True surrender to God . . . consists—according to the Fathers in fidelity to biblical thought—in the union of man and creation with God. Belonging to God . . . means losing oneself as the only possible way of finding oneself (Mark 8:35; Matt. 10:39). That is why St. Augustine could say that the true "sacrifice" is the *civitas Dei*, that is, love-transformed mankind, the divinization of creation and the surrender of all things to God: God all in all (1 Cor. 15:28). That is the purpose of the world. That is the essence of sacrifice and worship.

20. *Religions*, 68; *Beginning*, 29.
21. *Beginning*, 29–30.
22. *Liturgy*, 27.
23. *Liturgy*, 35.
24. *Ecumenism*, 198, 274.

And so we can now say that the goal of worship and the goal of creation as a whole are one and the same—divinization, a world of freedom and love. But this means that the historical makes its appearance in the cosmic. The cosmos is not a kind of closed building, a stationary container in which history may by chance take place. It is itself movement, from its one beginning to its one end. In a sense, creation *is* history.[25]

All of biblical history, as Benedict sees it, is ordered to the realization of the purposes of creation, which is the exalted and glorious state in which God will be "all in all." In sacrificial worship, men and women are made to share in the life of God and to cooperate in the accomplishment of their *theiosis*.

In Benedict's canonical reading, this beautiful vision is marred by the sin of the first man and woman. He affirms the ancient dogmatic and liturgical interpretation of Adam and Eve's "fall," although not without first considering how Israel's conflict with the ancient fertility cults influenced the final form of the text; he also notes the significant parallels between the story of the first couple's temptation and the accounts of Israel's temptations in the desert.[26]

These exegetical considerations lend nuance to his reading. He locates the origin of sin in "refusals and . . . doubt concerning God's covenant."[27] Sin, for Benedict, is essentially a selfish turning inward in which the person closes in on him- or herself, seeking to become "divine" and to realize happiness by his or her own means, apart from God's covenant of love.[28] Thus sin involves a distortion of freedom and the denial of the truth about the dialogic relation of God and the human person.

25. *Liturgy*, 28.
26. *Beginning*, 65–66.
27. *Beginning*, 77.
28. See Pope Benedict XVI, Message for Lent 2007 (November 21, 2006): "Unfortunately, from its very origins, mankind, seduced by the lies of the Evil One, rejected God's love in the illusion of a self-sufficiency that is impossible (compare Gen. 3:1–7). Turning in on himself, Adam withdrew from that source of life who is God himself, and became the first of 'those who through fear of death were subject to lifelong bondage' (Heb. 2:15)."

From the garden at Eden, biblical history moves toward the realization of God's plan in Jesus Christ. It is beyond our scope here to present even a partial picture of Benedict's canonical reading of the Old Testament. We can, however, say summarily that he reads the canonical text as a "great historical pilgrimage of the people of God"[29]—beginning with the call of Abraham, continuing through his sons, the patriarchs, and on to the revelation to Moses, the Exodus of Israel, and the covenant made at Mount Sinai. The promise made to David of "an everlasting kingdom" marks the final stage of the Old Testament, as the people of God await their Redeemer, who is to come in Jesus Christ.[30]

His reading of this history is characterized by an accent on the sacrificial-liturgical dimension of the covenant, a stress on the corporate and familial nature of God's redemptive plan, and a keen awareness of the "universalist" orientations written into the old covenant. The distinctive and foundational element of Benedict's biblical theology remains his insistence on the "indivisibility"[31] of the Old and New Testaments and on Jesus Christ and Christ's new-covenant Church as the true meaning and fulfillment of the economy of salvation, intended by God from the beginning.

Christology in the Unity of Law and Gospel

The figures of Christ and the Church stand at the heart of Benedict's biblical theology. In a certain sense, we might say that Benedict posits an ecclesiological culmination to the economy of salvation, but only if we keep in mind that Benedict's understanding of the Church is both profoundly christological and profoundly liturgical-sacramental. In Jesus and his Church, God's covenant plan of making all humanity into a divine family, a people of God, begins to be fulfilled. God's fidelity to this plan—announced in the

---

29. Pope Benedict XVI, Address to the Clergy of the Dioceses of Belluno-Feltre and Treviso (July 24, 2007).

30. *Pilgrim*, 270–71.

31. *Religions*, 28.

covenant with Abraham, renewed in the covenant with Israel at Sinai, and assured in the promises made to David—is revealed in Jesus and the founding of his Church, though it awaits its definitive consummation at the end of the age.[32]

Benedict rejects as unbiblical the sharp dialectic between Law and Gospel introduced by Martin Luther and presumed rather uncritically by the modern exegetical establishment.[33] By contrast, Benedict establishes from his close readings of the texts "the inner continuity and coherence of Law and Gospel" and the "deep unity between the good news of Jesus and the message of Sinai."[34] The hinge on which this unity depends is, again, the figure of Jesus Christ.

In his theological writings, Benedict sees Jesus at once as the Christ, the Messiah anticipated in the Old Testament texts;[35] the Torah of God made flesh;[36] the new and greater Moses;[37] the definitive David;[38] and the new Adam.[39] In these interpretative assertions, Benedict relies on solid historical and literary exegesis and judicious appropriation of patristic precedents. For instance, he reads the early christological hymn in Philippians 2:5–11 as an

32. "With Abraham's call, the story of the blessing begins: it is the beginning of God's great plan to make humanity one family through the covenant with a new people, chosen by him to be a blessing among all the peoples (compare Gen. 12:1–3). This divine plan is still being implemented; it culminated in the mystery of Christ. It was then that the 'last times' began, in the sense that the plan was fully revealed and brought about in Christ but needs to be accepted by human history, which always remains a history of fidelity on God's part, but unfortunately also of infidelity on the part of us human beings. The Church herself, the depository of the blessing, is holy and made up of sinners, marked by tension between the 'already' and the 'not yet.' In the fullness of time Jesus Christ came to bring the covenant to completion: he himself, true God and true man, is the sacrament of God's fidelity to his plan of salvation for all humanity, for all of us" (Pope Benedict XVI, Homily, Solemnity of the Epiphany of the Lord [January 6, 2008]).

33. On Benedict's rejection of this dialectic, see "Interpretation," 250–51 and Joseph Cardinal Ratzinger, "The Renewal of Moral Theology: Perspectives of Vatican II and *Veritatis Splendor*," *Communio* 32, no. 2 (2005): 357–68, esp. 360.

34. *Religions*, 33, 36.

35. *Way*, 57.

36. *Beginning*, 30; *Religions*, 70; *Jesus*, 110–11.

37. *Jesus*, 66.

38. *Dogma*, 23.

39. *Beginning*, 49.

allusion to the story of Adam.[40] He finds good critical grounds
for accepting the Fathers' allegorical interpretation of the parables
of the Good Samaritan and the Prodigal Son as also referring to
Adam.[41] As we will see in the chapters to come, his readings of the
Last Supper and the crucifixion are likewise built on an acceptance
of typological interpretations.

He makes a careful comparison of the genealogies of Jesus
in Matthew and Luke to illuminate the twin aspects of Christ's
soteriological project. By tracing Jesus' lineage to Abraham, Matthew highlights God's faithfulness to his covenant promises to the
patriarch and especially to David. Luke's genealogy, which embeds
Jesus in a line descending from "Adam, son of God" (3:38), establishes that Jesus' mission transcends ethnicity and nationality.
As Benedict interprets this, "In Jesus Christ the creation of man
first attains its true goal; in him the Creator's conception of man
finds its full expression."[42]

It is not possible here to do justice to Benedict's important
contributions to biblical Christology. It is enough for our purposes
that we acknowledge that he has made a compelling scholarly case
for trusting the biblical portrait of Jesus as Messiah ("Christ"),
Lord, and Son of God. And we must note, as he does in concluding
his detailed exegesis in *Jesus of Nazareth*, that the christological
titles found in the New Testament are all "deeply rooted . . . in
the Word of God, Israel's Bible, the Old Testament. And yet all
these terms receive their full meaning only in him; *it is as if they
had been waiting for him.*"[43]

Here we must recognize again the value of typology in Benedict's
project. "It is not at all unusual for different typological connections to converge in the events occurring along Jesus' way. This
makes it plain that Moses and the prophets all speak of Jesus."[44]
While granting that typology has been excessively and inappro-

40. *Pilgrim*, 168; Pope Benedict XVI, Homily, Holy Mass with the Members of
the Bishops' Conference of Switzerland (November 7, 2006).
41. *Jesus*, 199–200, 205–6; *Way*, 86.
42. *Dogma*, 22.
43. *Jesus*, 354; emphasis added.
44. *Jesus*, 308.

priately applied at times in the history of interpretation, Benedict nonetheless affirms:

> But the central and quite justified significance, the essential message of typology is absolutely right here: there is a line running right through the history of faith and worship. Inwardly, things correspond to this—there are deviations, but there is also a path in a particular direction: the inner harmony with the figure of Jesus Christ, with his message and his existence, simply cannot be ruled out, in spite of the variety of historical contexts and stages. . . . Christ is moving through history in these forms and figures, as (again with the Fathers) we may express it.[45]

The Preaching of the Kingdom and the Identity of the Church

At the center of Jesus' preaching and mission is the kingdom of God. Benedict has done a great deal of work in this area, which, along with debate over the historical Jesus, is among the most contentious domains of New Testament scholarship. As with his Christology, we can only glance here at his larger work of kingdom ecclesiology, keeping in mind that our aim is to sketch the fundamentals of his overall biblical theology and to see how his theological method opens new doors for understanding the content of the faith.

In this biblical theology, the identity of the kingdom and the relationship of the kingdom to Christ and to the Church are crucial. Benedict openly confronts the famous barbed quip of Alfred Loisy, the modernist exegete: "Jesus proclaimed the Kingdom; what came was the Church."[46] Benedict sees the presumed dialectic of Church and kingdom as another artificial byproduct of the erroneous philosophy that underlies the historical-critical method. His response is calm and simple: "A historical reading of the texts reveals that the opposition of Kingdom and Church has no factual basis."[47]

45. *Truth*, 97.
46. *Eschatology*, 24. See also *Jesus*, 48–49.
47. *Communion*, 21.

While he rejects the individualist and political interpretations of the kingdom common in the modern era, he also seems intent not to be drawn into superficial peripheral debates about whether or to what extent the Church on earth can be identified with the kingdom. That said, his ecclesiological work presumes a deep interpenetration of Church and kingdom and presumes the Catholic Church to be at the summit of the divine economy written into the pages of the Old and the New Testaments.

At times his language regarding the kingdom is indistinguishable from his language regarding the Church. Thus he can identify, using statistical analyses and word studies, the kingdom as "the true *Leitmotiv* of Jesus' preaching"[48] and as "the foundation of the Church, and thus the realization of Christ's mission."[49]

As Benedict reads it, the kingdom of God in Jesus' preaching means not a temporal institutional monarchy but something far greater: the reign of the living God over all creation, God's sovereign presence in the world established finally and forever, his command as King and Lord.

> When Jesus speaks of the Kingdom of God, he is quite simply proclaiming God, and proclaiming him to be the living God, who is able to act concretely in the world and in history and is even now so acting. . . . The new and totally specific thing about his message is that he is telling us: God is acting now—this is the hour when God is showing himself in history as its Lord, as the living God, as the way that goes beyond anything seen before. "Kingdom of God" is therefore an inadequate translation. It would be better to speak of God's being-Lord, of his lordship. . . . The announcement of God's lordship is, like Jesus' entire message, founded on the Old Testament. Jesus reads the Old Testament, in its progressive movement from the beginnings with Abraham right down to his own time, as a single whole; precisely when we grasp this movement as a whole, we see that it leads directly to Jesus himself.[50]

48. *Jesus*, 48.
49. Joseph Cardinal Ratzinger, *The Meaning of Christian Brotherhood* (San Francisco: Ignatius, 1993 [1960]), 75.
50. *Jesus*, 55–56.

The identity of Jesus as the Davidic "son" of God, the royal son promised to David (2 Sam. 7:12–13) is vital to Benedict's understanding of the Church and the kingdom. In his detailed treatment in *Jesus of Nazareth*, he notes that the christological title of Son reflects a long development of thought in the Old Testament. In the covenant, Israel is regarded as God's "firstborn son" (Exod. 4:22). By the time of the Davidic kingdom, the king was "personified" as God's firstborn son. The application of the title to Jesus in the apostolic preaching reflects hopes expressed later in the Old Testament for a Davidic son, "the king who was to come."[51] The New Testament understands Jesus as that long-awaited "true king of the world."[52] He embodies the dynamic thrust of the Old Testament, which, from the call of Abraham onward, envisions a universal gathering of Israel and the nations under the lordship of God.[53]

Benedict's theology presumes a certain historical trajectory in the biblical narrative. He illuminates a strain of prophetic expectation in which Israel's hopes for restoration from exile and the reestablishment of the Davidic kingdom at Zion are described as an eschatological "gathering" of the children of God scattered among the nations.[54] Jesus himself alludes to this expectation, and Benedict often uses the word "gathering" to characterize the essence of this mission: "For he came in order to gather together what was dispersed (see John 11:52; Matt. 12:30). His entire work is thus to gather the new people."[55]

Jesus' gospel of the kingdom is seen as the fulfillment of the promise inherent in the old covenant. It is pivotal for Benedict's

51. See the full discussion in *Jesus*, 335–45.
52. *Dogma*, 23.
53. See *Religions*, 28: "The Old and New Testaments, Jesus and the Holy Scriptures of Israel, appear inseparably joined together. The new dynamism of Jesus' mission, the bringing of Israel and the nations into unity, corresponds to the prophetic dynamism of the Old Testament itself. Reconciliation, which takes place in the common acknowledgement that God is king and that his will is our way, is the core of Jesus' mission. And in his mission, the person and the message are inseparable." See also *Catechism*, 79.
54. See, for example, Isa. 11:12; 13:4; Jer. 3:17; 23:3; Ezek. 34:13, 23.
55. *Communion*, 23.

interpretation that the covenant with Abraham, which established the people of God, was universalist in its intention—promising that all the nations of the world would be blessed through Abraham's family.[56] "With Jesus Christ, Abraham's blessing was extended to all peoples, to the universal Church as the new Israel which welcomes within her the whole of humanity."[57]

Here we glimpse the inseparability of Church and kingdom and the Church's essential continuity with the people of God, Israel. The calling of the twelve apostles is an obvious symbolic allusion to the patriarchal structure of Israel and the twelve sons of Jacob. As Benedict says, this calling must be "understood in the light of [God's] special relationship with Israel, the community of the Covenant, in continuity with the history of salvation."[58] The kingdom that Jesus announces is the new family of God, the new Israel.[59]

Drawing again from historical and exegetical research, he observes both Abrahamic and Davidic notes in Christ's authority structure for this new people of God. Establishing Peter's primacy among the apostles, Jesus designates him as a "rock," alluding to biblical and rabbinic characterizations of Abraham's faith as the solid rock of Israel's foundation. In the same passage (Matt. 16:18–19), Jesus gives Peter "the keys" of the kingdom, which is a clear reference to a prophetic tradition regarding authority and succession in the kingdom of David.[60]

56. See Gen. 22:17–18; *Religions*, 68.
57. Homily, Solemnity of the Epiphany of the Lord (January 6, 2008). See also *Jesus*, 325: "In the Son of Man, man is revealed as he truly ought to be."
58. *Jesus*, 65–67; Pope Benedict XVI, General Audience (March 15, 2006).
59. Among the several images for the Church that we find in Jesus' preaching, the image of "the family of God" is clearly Jesus' "favorite," according to Benedict. "God is the father of the family, Jesus the master of the house, and it therefore stands to reason that he addresses the members of this people as children, even though they are adults, and that to gain true understanding of themselves, those who belong to this people must first lay down their grown-up autonomy and acknowledge themselves as children before God (compare Mark 10:24; Matt. 11:25)" (*Communion*, 23–24). See also his discussion in terms of the "family" structure of the Passover and the Last Supper in *Pierced*, 105: "Jesus too celebrated the Passover . . . at home with his family; that is to say, with the apostles, who had become his new family. . . . That is how the Passover became a Christian feast. We are Christ's *ḥabhûrâ*, his family. . . . Thus, the Church is new family."
60. See the discussion in *Communion*, 53–65.

Benedict also notes something many scholars overlook. There is a cultic and liturgical character to the apostolic office. The odd-sounding phrase in the Gospel of Mark—literally, "he *made* twelve" (3:14)—is used in the Old Testament for the appointment of priests. The leaders of the Church are, then, in the literal historical sense of the text being established by Jesus as both prophets and priests in continuity with the Old Testament tradition.[61]

The New Qahal and the Covenant People of God

Benedict also sees important lines of continuity between Israel's Sinai covenant traditions and the Church's cultic and liturgical character. For him, there is deep significance in the fact that the New Testament word for "church" (*ecclesia*) is used in the Septuagint to translate *qahal*, the liturgical assembly of the people of God. The original purposes of the *qahal* were cultic: to remember and renew the covenant made at Sinai. Again Benedict stresses the nature of the covenant as a forging of kinship bonds: "The assembly at Sinai goes beyond the Word: in the covenant, it united God and man in a kind of community of blood, as blood relations, symbolically represented there, which is the heart of the 'covenant.'"[62]

Jesus, in establishing the Eucharist as the heart of his new covenant (see Mark 14:24), evoked the "blood of the covenant" at Sinai. We will explore this more in the next chapter. Here it is important to note that in the years of Israel's exile and division—which extended into the time of Christ—the restoration of the *qahal* "increasingly became the center of Jewish hope."

> The supplication for this gathering—for the appearance of the *ecclesia*—is a fixed component of late Jewish prayer. It is thus clear what it means for the nascent Church to call herself *ecclesia*. By doing so, she says in effect: This petition is granted in us. Christ,

---

61. Cf. Mark 3:14; 1 Kings 12:31; 13:33; *Jesus*, 171. On the importance of the image of the twelve, see *Communion*, 25–26. On the priesthood of Jesus, which we will consider more in the next chapter, see *Jesus*, 302.
62. *Pilgrim*, 105.

who died and rose again, is the living Sinai; those who approach him
are the chosen final gathering of God's people (see Heb. 12:18–24).
. . . The self-description of the new people as *ecclesia* defines it in
terms both of the continuity of the covenant in saving history and
of the newness of the mystery of Christ, which is open to what
lies ahead.[63]

The Church, then, is the new *qahal*, the new covenant people
of God and "the path by which God intends to come to all men."[64]
All the strands of Benedict's ecclesiology of salvation are drawn
together in his interpretation of the Pentecost event (Acts 2). If the
resurrection revealed once and for all the true identity of Christ,
then the sending of his Spirit at Pentecost reveals the true nature
of the Church and its purpose in the divine economy.

Benedict notes first the Old Testament significance of this feast,
which the Jews celebrated fifty days after Passover. For Israel, it
was a festival commemorating the covenant made at Sinai. For
the nascent Church, it would become the feast of the new covenant. As the covenant at Sinai was accompanied by wind and fire
(Exod. 19:16–19), these elements—perhaps indicators of a "new
creation"—are present too in the upper room at Jerusalem.

The repetition of the number twelve in the Pentecost narrative
is a key to its interpretation, as is the presence of pilgrims from
"every nation under heaven" (Acts 2:5). The newly reconstituted
college of twelve apostles is there, suggesting that Luke intends
to signify the Church as a "new Israel . . . an authentic *qahal*, an
'assembly' in accordance with the model of the first covenant, the
community summoned to listen to the Lord's voice and walk in
his ways."[65]

Luke lists the presence of people from exactly twelve countries
or regions, apparently drawing from a list compiled under Alex-
ander the Great intended to be representative of all the peoples of
the world. This symbolism of twelve, related to the cosmic symbol

63. *Communion*, 30–32.
64. *Jesus*, 22.
65. Pope Benedict XVI, Homily, Eucharistic Celebration on the Solemnity of Pentecost (May 11, 2008).

of the twelve constellations, is meant to convey the sense of the Church's "catholic"—meaning universal—mission.

Another "catholic" sign in the text is the way the apostolic preaching is understood in his or her native tongue by each person present. Benedict sees this as an echo of the biblical story of the confusion of tongues at the tower of Babel (Gen. 11:1–9). Stressing the etymology of the Greek word translated "catholic," he says the point of "the wonderful gift of languages" is to illustrate "that the Church is *kat'holon* from the very first moment—comprehending the whole universe."[66]

Benedict notes that in addition to the list of twelve nations, Luke identifies a delegation present from Rome as well. Rome, of course, is the imperial capital and hence another symbol of the whole world. Indeed, as Benedict stresses, Luke's narrative in Acts begins in Jerusalem and concludes in Rome with Paul preaching the gospel there (Acts 28:30–31). This movement is an expression of God's "providential plan" and represents the notion of the gospel having been preached "to the ends of the earth" (Acts 1:8).[67]

Hence in Acts we have what Benedict describes as "narrative ecclesiology."[68] The text is structured in such a way as to reveal "a dynamic view of the Church's role in salvation history, in which the dimension of catholicity is essential. Finally, it is a *liturgical ecclesiology*: the gathered community receives the gifts of the Spirit in the act of prayer."[69]

---

66. *Pilgrim*, 136–37.

67. Homily, Solemnity of Pentecost (May 11, 2008).

68. *Communion*, 41; see also 45: "The whole book of Acts is arranged, not according to purely historiographical concerns, but on the basis of a theological idea. It portrays the path of the Gospel from the Jews to the Gentiles and thus depicts the fulfillment of the commission with which Jesus left his disciples: to be his witnesses 'to the ends of the earth' (Acts 1:8). However, in the general plan of the book, the path of the witnesses—in particular of St. Paul—from Jerusalem to Rome becomes in turn a graphic synthesis of this theological way. In Luke's presentation, Rome is the recapitulation of the pagan world as such." See also *Pierced*, 73.

69. *Pierced*, 73–74; emphasis added. See also *Pilgrim*, 62: "With the arrival in Rome, the journey begun in Jerusalem has reached its goal; the universal—the catholic— Church has come into being, continuing the old chosen People of God and taking over its history, its mission."

The Davidic Dynasty and the Kingship of God

In the Church, the mission of Israel, the promise of the Old Covenant, is brought to fruition. Jesus, in continuity with those promises, affirmed that "salvation is from the Jews" (John 4:22). Through Christ and the Church, the divine Word first spoken only to the Jews is now spoken to all humankind.[70] The God who revealed himself first to Israel now addresses all men and women, of every race and nationality, calling them to communion in the Church, the new family of God in which they will find "filial communion with the Father."[71]

> The mission of Jesus is to unite Jews and pagans into a single people of God in which the universalist promises of the Scriptures are fulfilled that speak again and again of the nations worshipping the God of Israel. . . . The mission of Jesus consists in bringing together the histories of the nations in a common sharing in the history of Abraham, which is the history of Israel. . . . The history of Israel is destined to become the history of all men, Abrahamic sonship is meant to be extended to the "many." . . . All nations . . . become brothers and receivers of the promises of the chosen people; they become the people of God together with Israel through adherence to the will of God and through their acceptance of the Davidic kingdom.[72]

Here Benedict alludes to the final covenant of the Old Testament, namely, God's covenant with David and his promise to establish David's house as an everlasting kingdom (2 Sam. 7:11–16; 23:5; Ps. 89). The Davidic-dynastic covenant is at the center of the "element of promise and . . . hopeful expectation" that characterizes the "faith of Israel" at the time of Jesus. As Benedict reads Israel's history, "Davidic 'court theology'" is the source of Israel's hope for "the Messiah, a king of David's lineage who would shape the kingdom of Israel into its perfected form."[73]

70. *Catechism*, 79.
71. *Jesus*, 117; see also 290.
72. *Religions*, 26–28. See also *Catechism*, 78–79.
73. *Eschatology*, 27.

Yet he also notes that in the prophets there grows an apocalyptic hope for God's decisive entrance into the world to establish his rule through a divine "mediator." Daniel envisions God exercising power through the figure of the Son of Man; Isaiah foresees a "servant" of God; and Zechariah anticipates a priestly and kingly Messiah. Yet there persisted also a political formulation of the "Davidic national idea," as seen in the Zealot party and various messianic aspirants.[74]

Benedict's Christology and ecclesiology presumes this diversified Old Testament background. His ecclesiology is likewise informed by a rich understanding of the Mother of Christ as the personification of Zion, the eschatological kingdom of David.[75]

As we have mentioned, Benedict finds in the New Testament the strong belief that Jesus is the "true David."[76] This belief is encoded in the genealogy that serves as the introduction to the New Testament. Benedict notices, as many ancient commentators did, that the genealogy is composed of three sections of fourteen names each. The number fourteen, in turn, if written in Hebrew letters, forms the three consonants that make up the name "David."

> Thus the number fourteen, which dominates the genealogy, is a symbol of kingship. It turns the genealogy into a royal genealogy in which not only is the promise to Abraham fulfilled but the promise as well that accompanies the name of David. The meaning is that the One who is coming is the true King of the world.[77]

74. See the discussion in *Eschatology*, 24–28.
75. "She is in person the true Zion, toward whom hopes have yearned throughout all the devastations of history. She *is* the true Israel in whom old and new covenant, Israel and Church, are indivisibly one. She is the 'people of God' bearing fruit through God's gracious power" (Joseph Cardinal Ratzinger, *Daughter Zion: Meditations on the Church's Marian Belief*, trans. John M. McDermott [San Francisco: Ignatius, 1983 (1977)], 43). This is not the place for a presentation of Benedict's Mariology. But it is important to note that Mary has a central role in Benedict's understanding of salvation history. Suggestive lines of biblical-theological inquiry are opened up in his discussion of the biblical establishment of Mary as "mother" of the new family of God (see *Co-Workers*, 319). For Benedict, Mary "carries within her the whole mystery of the Church" (*Pilgrim*, 151).
76. Ratzinger, *Daughter Zion*, 40.
77. *Dogma*, 23.

Benedict acknowledges that because they began with a "royal genealogy," the New Testament writers see God's promise to David "as being fulfilled in Jesus the Son of David."[78] At the same time, Benedict is aware that the New Testament bears witness to the fact that many, if not most, of Jesus' contemporaries misunderstood the true nature of his preaching of the kingdom. We see this confusion even among Jesus' apostles (see Acts 1:6).

Many, like the Zealots, were expecting the restoration of an earthly and political kingdom to be brought about by revolutionary means. Benedict brings this out in his discussion of the trial of Jesus. The figure of Barabbas, he notes, is not simply a common criminal. The term used to describe Barabbas, often translated "robber," actually has a political meaning.[79] Barabbas would appear to be a revolutionary and a messianic figure seeking to establish an earthly kingdom of God by violent political action. Noting that his name, "Bar-Abbas," means "Son of the Father," Benedict suggests that he is presented in the Gospels as "a kind of *doppelgänger* [double] for Jesus."[80]

Barabbas, then, represents those who would interpret the restoration of the Davidic kingdom in political and nationalistic terms. But the kingdom of the true David is not of this world. It is not political but spiritual, not national but international. Benedict sees in Jesus the convergence of the numerous lines of Old Testament expectation. Jesus is establishing a kingdom, but he is also establishing the direct rule of God. "His kingdom is the Kingdom of God himself; it shares in the universality of God's rule, since in his person God himself has stepped into the history of the world."[81] The promise of the New Testament, the basic datum of Christology and ecclesiology, lies in this: "that Jesus is a son of David, the promised heir who will uphold the Davidic dynasty and will transform its kingdom into a kingship of God over all the world."[82]

78. Joseph Cardinal Ratzinger, *God and the World: A Conversation with Peter Seewald*, trans. Henry Taylor (San Francisco: Ignatius, 2002 [2000]), 208.
79. See Matt. 27:16; Luke 23:19, 25; John 18:40.
80. *Way*, 97.
81. *Eucharist*, 15–16.
82. *Eucharist*, 15–16.

If Christ is the true David, the one in whom the Davidic promise of the kingdom is being fulfilled, then it follows that the kingdom proclaimed by Christ must in some sense be understood as the restored and renewed Davidic kingdom. Here we begin to better understand the true relationship of essential unity that Benedict sees between kingdom and Church.

Loisy was right. There is a marked difference between the preaching of Jesus, which was centered on the kingdom, and the post-Easter proclamation of the Church, which was centered on Christ. Loisy's mistake, in which he was followed by generations of theologians and exegetes, was to see in that difference a sign of rupture or contradiction.

Recasting Loisy's jibe, Benedict says, "The Kingdom was promised and what came was Jesus."[83] The Church's proclamation of Jesus was faithful to his preaching. In other words, Jesus was the kingdom he announced.[84] Church and kingdom, the gathering of the eschatological people of God, are one in the person of Jesus Christ, in his presence in the Eucharist until the end of the age. For this reason, Benedict concludes that Loisy's question is really the wrong one. "The basic question is actually about the relationship between the Kingdom of God and Christ. It is on this that our understanding of the Church will depend."[85]

The authentic historical continuity between the Church and Israel grounds this sacramental understanding of the Church. Failure to see in Christ the unity of Church and kingdom is a failure "to recognize that not only [that] Jesus stands within the salvation history of the Jewish people, but also his intention to renew this people, indeed, to renew salvation history as a whole, to make it broader and more profound—and thereby to create what we call the Church."[86]

Thus we are able to see that for Benedict the divine economy revealed in sacred Scripture begins and ends in the Church. The Church is "God's great idea,"[87] the agent for the final realization

83. *Communion*, 21–23; see also 142.
84. See the discussion in *Eschatology*, 25.
85. *Jesus*, 49.
86. Ratzinger, *God and the World*, 344.
87. *Pilgrim*, 135.

of his plan for creation in the beginning. In this the Church is the fulfillment of the Old Testament idea of Israel, existing not for her own sake but for the sake of God's covenant will for creation.

> In the writings of the Fathers, the one and only Church precedes creation. . . . Here the Fathers are continuing a theme of rabbinic theology by which the Torah and Israel had been conceived of as being preexistent. . . . Since the Fathers were fully persuaded that Israel and the Church were ultimately identical, they could not regard the Church as something that came into being at a late hour, by chance, but recognized in this gathering of the nations under the will of God the inner goal of creation.[88]

88. *Pilgrim*, 134.

7

The Embrace of Salvation

Mystagogy and the Transformation of Sacrifice

The Church Subsists as Liturgy and in the Liturgy

In Benedict's reading of salvation history, creation exists for Christ and for his Church. What the rabbis believed about the Torah and Israel, the New Testament writers and the Church Fathers believed about the Church, namely, that it was preexistent, that before the world was made there was the Church. This belief in the "ontological precedence of the Church" can be seen in the book of Revelation and in the Pauline letters, such as Ephesians and Colossians. But it is also present in the theology of Paul, who spoke of "the Jerusalem above . . . our mother" (Gal. 4:26).

For Benedict as well, the Church—the new Israel—was not an afterthought in the divine plan but the forethought, the very reason for salvation history. Indeed, he agrees with what he describes as the testimony of the Fathers: that "Israel and the Church [are] ultimately identical" and that the Church, as the final "gathering of the nations under the will of God," is "the inner goal of creation."[1]

1. See the discussion in *Pilgrim*, 134–36.

At the heart of his biblical theology lies a "dynamic ecclesiology of salvation history, of which the dimension of catholicity is
an essential part."[2] This finding has implications both for how we
interpret the Bible and for how we understand the Church and its
relationship to history. "Christ and *ecclesia* are the hermeneutical
center of the scriptural narration of the history of God's saving
dealings with man."[3]

This history of God's salvific dealings with humanity did not
end with the coming of the Church. The Church is not the end of
salvation history but rather its decisive fulfillment and opening
to the "last days," the eschatological future. As the inner goal of
history, the Church has "already" arrived but "not yet" completely.
The definitive divine ingathering has begun, but it is still being
worked out in history, which is now in the age of the Church. The
new covenant has been made in the blood of Christ shed on the
cross. That new covenant, which is the salvation of the many, is
being offered to all nations in the preaching and the sacraments
of the Church. This will continue until Christ returns for the final
gathering of his kingdom.

The Church, established by Jesus on the basis of his new interpretation of the Old Testament and on the sacrament of the
Eucharist, is the realization "in practice" of the kingdom he proclaimed.[4] The Church is the kingdom, the people gathered by
faith in the salvific event of the cross, remembered and renewed in
the liturgy of the Eucharist. At the heart of that kingdom, then,
are cross and Eucharist. Indeed, cross and Eucharist form a single
"paschal mystery" that "sums up God's love story with man."[5]

> The Eucharist reveals the loving plan that guides all of salvation his-
> tory (Eph. 1:10; 3:8–11). There the *Deus Trinitas*, who is essentially
> love (1 John 4:7–8), becomes fully a part of our human condition.
> In the bread and wine under whose appearances Christ gives himself

2. *Pilgrim*, 63.
3. Joseph Cardinal Ratzinger and Hans Urs von Balthasar, *Mary: The Church at
the Source*, trans. Adrian Walker (San Francisco: Ignatius, 1997), 30.
4. *Pilgrim*, 146.
5. *Pierced*, 61.

to us in the paschal meal (Luke 22:14–20; 1 Cor. 11:23–26), God's whole life encounters us and is sacramentally shared with us.[6]

The world was made in the beginning for this ultimate encounter with the living God, the Trinity, in the Church. And the world's encounter with the Trinity takes place in the liturgy of the new covenant, the eucharistic liturgy of the Church, in which we have real contact with the paschal mystery of Christ. Hence the eucharistic liturgy is pivotal in Benedict's biblical theology. The liturgy is far more than something the Church *does*, a set of ritual words and actions it performs. The liturgy is, in a very real sense, what the Church *is*. And as we will see more fully in the next two chapters, everything in the Church is ordered toward the liturgical gathering and purification of humankind and serves to prepare us for the consummation of history in the divine liturgy of the cosmos.

> The Church is there, not for her own sake, but for mankind. She is there so that the world may become a sphere for God's presence, the sphere of the covenant between God and men. Thus, that is what the creation story is saying (Gen. 1:1–2:4): the way that the text moves toward the Sabbath is trying to make clear that creation has an inner basis and purpose. It is there in order that the covenant may come to be in which God freely gives his love and receives the response of love.[7]

The sphere of the covenant is what we described in the last chapter as the *theiosis* of humankind. This divinization—this union of God and humanity in which God is "all in all" (1 Cor. 15:28)[8]—will not finally be realized until the end of the age. Yet it is anticipated and in some fashion accomplished in every celebration of the Eucharist.

This deep understanding of the liturgical nature of the Church and the liturgical teleology of history gives Benedict's biblical

6. Pope Benedict XVI, *Sacramentum Caritatis*, Post-Synodal Apostolic Exhortation on the Eucharist as the Source and Summit of the Church's Life and Mission (February 22, 2007), 8.
7. *Pilgrim*, 287–88.
8. *Benedict XVI*, 149.

theology a strongly *mystagogical* quality. In the early Church, the term "mystagogy" referred to explaining the sacraments in light of the biblical events of salvation history. Paul's account of baptism and the Eucharist as being typologically anticipated in Israel's Exodus and Peter's description of baptism as a type of the great flood are examples of primitive mystagogy.[9]

But mystagogy means more than simply conveying information about the sacraments. Mystagogy means leading believers into a real participation in the very salvific mysteries celebrated in the symbols and rituals of the liturgy. "The mature fruit of mystagogy is an awareness that one's life is being progressively transformed by the holy mysteries being celebrated . . . mak[ing] him a 'new creation.'"[10] Thus mystagogy is rooted in the transformative power of the divine Word. In the Gospels, Christ's Word brought about the realities it signified. He spoke and demons were cast out, people were healed, raging winds and waters were stilled, and the dead were raised. That same divine Word, spoken in the Church's liturgy, is likewise "performative," as we will see when we discuss the Mass in the next chapter.[11]

In his concern for mystagogy, we again see the deep influence of the Church Fathers on Benedict's thought and temperament. With the Fathers, he sees the divine economy continuing in the Church's sacramental liturgy. We enter into the salvation offered by Christ through the liturgy, which is an encounter with his life-changing Word:

> The liturgy is the privileged place in which to hear the divine Word which makes present the Lord's saving acts; but it is also the context in which the community raises its prayer celebrating divine love. God and man meet each other in an embrace of salvation that finds fulfillment precisely in the liturgical celebration. We might say that

9. See 1 Cor. 10:1–4; 1 Pet. 3:20–21. On mystagogy, see Scott Hahn, *Letter and Spirit: From Written Text to Living Word in the Liturgy* (New York: Doubleday, 2005), 25–32.

10. Benedict XVI, *Sacramentum Caritatis*, 65.

11. See Pope Benedict XVI, *Spe Salvi*, Encyclical Letter on Christian Hope (November 30, 2007), 2; *Jesus*, 47.

this is almost a definition of the liturgy: it brings about an embrace of salvation between God and man.[12]

This understanding leads to a eucharistic ecclesiology or an ecclesiology of communion. "The Church is effectively realized in the eucharistic celebration in which the Word of preaching likewise becomes present."[13] The prayer of the Church becomes a participation in the love of God poured out on the cross. "We are the people of God in no other way than on the basis of the crucified and risen body of Christ."[14]

Again note the normative importance of New Testament witness for Benedict's biblical theology. The departure point for Benedict's *communio* or eucharistic ecclesiology can be found in the simple description of the Church at Jerusalem in the days after the resurrection and ascension of Christ: "They devoted themselves to the apostles' teaching and fellowship [Greek: *koinonia*, or communion], to the breaking of bread and the prayers" (Acts 2:42; cf. Luke 24:35).

We can see in this a sketch of the primitive Christian service of worship, which starts with the teaching of the apostles, that is, with the proclamation and hearing of the faith of the Church, of the Word of God that is alive in her and that thus becomes the basis for liturgical and living fellowship: it reaches a climax in the eucharistic encounter with the Lord, who gives himself to us as bread, and resounds in songs of praise. The Church is adoration. This passage is telling us that the Church subsists as *liturgy* and in *liturgy*. She is the living temple that, even within the stone Temple in Jerusalem, dedicated to destruction, is growing up on the foundation stone of Christ."[15]

12. Pope Benedict XVI, General Audience (October 5, 2005). See also General Audience (June 27, 2007).
13. *Communion*, 77.
14. *Ecumenism*, 19. See also *Principles*, 55.
15. *Eucharist*, 121–22. In saying that the Church *subsists as* liturgy and *in* liturgy, Benedict appears to be deliberately employing the language that the Second Vatican Council adopted to describe how the Church of Jesus Christ is related to the visible organization called the Catholic Church. For Benedict's discussion of the ecclesiological issues involved in the Latin term *subsistit*, see *Pilgrim*, 144–49; *Benedict XVI*, 97–100.

The Church, in its essence, can be seen most clearly *in* the liturgy and *as* the liturgy. Hence Benedict can state boldly: "The Church *is* the Eucharist."[16] The Church *is* prayer. The Church exists to adore and glorify God. The Church exists to be that place on earth—in time and history—in which the living God is worshiped and glorified in Spirit and in truth.

The Church is built up in the celebration of the Eucharist, as men and women are made one body with Christ in their communion with his body and blood. This makes the Church a *communio* and the *corpus Christi*. Each of these images is intended to convey the gift of *koinonia*, the communion with the living God brought about by the Eucharist. And this means that theology must always be, in some way, Christology and ecclesiology and that it must also be a liturgical, or sacramental, theology. "The Church derives from adoration, from the task of glorifying God. Ecclesiology, of its nature, has to do with liturgy."[17]

The purpose of the assembly, of the Church, is worship. Thus Benedict sees a continuity between the *ecclesia* and the *qahal*. The community of Sinai is the "archetype" of the Church. "They come together to hear God's Word and to seal everything with sacrifice. That is how a 'covenant' is established between God and man."[18] As we will see, the eucharistic assembly of the Church likewise serves for the renewal of the new covenant, through the hearing of God's Word and the offering of sacrifice.

Benedict also again reminds us that the priesthood is at the heart of the Church. In the last chapter, we considered his understanding of the essential priestly character of the apostolic office.[19] Following the exegesis of St. Cyril of Jerusalem, Benedict points out that in Scripture the first appearance of the word *ecclesia* is in connection with Aaron's investiture as high priest. "Priesthood and the Church come to birth together and belong together indivisibly. To describe the Church is therefore at the same time to explain what is the heart and the meaning of the priestly task: *They devoted*

16. *Pilgrim*, 103; see also 105.
17. *Pilgrim*, 126.
18. *Liturgy*, 63.
19. *Song*, 175.

themselves to the apostles' teaching and fellowship, to the breaking of the bread and the prayers."[20]

The Whole of Christology

The priestly and liturgical character of the people of God flows directly from the inner logic of Jesus' own life. This brings us to one of Benedict's most unique and important contributions to Christology: his emphasis on the prayer of Jesus, that is, that "the center of the person of Jesus is prayer."[21]

In his important essay, "Taking Bearings in Christology,"[22] Benedict demonstrates that the New Testament portrait of Jesus is that of a person in constant prayer. The prayer of Jesus is not abstract or monologic. Rather, the prayer of Jesus is an intimate, intense, and sustained dialogue with the God he calls "Father." The Church's earliest confessions and hymns, which profess faith in Jesus as the Son of God, only confirm the witness of the apostles and the testimony of the Scriptures—that Jesus lived in unbroken "primal conversation with the Father."[23]

The Father that Jesus prayed to was "the God of the fathers," the patriarchs of Israel,[24] and Jesus prayed as a child of these

20. *Eucharist*, 122–23; emphasis added. See Lev. 8:3; Cyril of Jerusalem, *Catechetical Lectures* 18.24; *Liturgy*, 63.

21. *Pierced*, 25. As I noted earlier, unfortunately I cannot do justice to Benedict's Christology within the scope of these efforts to sketch the fundamentals of his biblical theology. I would, however, like to suggest that several lifetimes worth of study and prayer are opened up by his observation that "*the whole of Christology*—our speaking of Christ—*is nothing other than the interpretation of his prayer*: the entire person of Jesus is contained in his prayer" (*Pierced*, 20; emphasis added). See also *Faith*, 26–27: "A fundamental word in the mouth of 'the Son' is 'Abba.' It is no accident that we find this word characterizing the figure of Jesus in the New Testament. It expresses his whole being, and all that he says to God in prayer is ultimately only an explication of his being (and hence an explication of this one word): the 'Our Father' is this same 'Abba' transposed into the plural for the benefit of those who are his."

22. In *Pierced*, 13–46. This essay has been republished in its entirety as "Seven Theses on Christology and the Hermeneutic of Faith," *Letter & Spirit* 3 (2007): 189–209.

23. *Pierced*, 32. This, too, is a very fruitful insight for exegesis and dogmatic theology, although we cannot develop it here.

24. See, for instance, Exod. 3:13, 15–16.

patriarchs, as a son of Abraham. He was part of this ancient family, this people of God. This, too, is vital to Benedict's theological understanding. Jesus prayed with his people, in conversation with the Scriptures of Israel, as is vividly depicted in the Transfiguration, where he talks personally with Moses and the prophet Elijah.[25]

Jesus also participated in the liturgy, Israel's corporate prayer. Indeed, especially in John, the calendar of Jewish feasts provides the structure for Jesus' life. But these feasts serve as more than markers or background information in John's narrative. There is a very dynamic sense in which Jesus is being portrayed as almost the embodiment of the *qahal*, Israel's covenantal-liturgical assembly; his life is seen as a lived liturgy. As Benedict says, "The great events of Jesus' life are inwardly connected with the Jewish festival calendar. They are, as it were, liturgical events in which the liturgy, with its remembrance and expectation, becomes reality—becomes life. This life then leads back to the liturgy and from the liturgy seeks to become life again."[26]

At the heart of Christ's life as portrayed in the Gospels is his journey to his final Passover, celebrated in the days before his death. Here the prayer of Jesus becomes a kind of typological interpretation of the whole Old Testament. "The exodus of Israel and the exodus of Jesus touch each other: all the feasts and all the ways of Israel lead to the passover of Jesus Christ."[27]

Jesus' exodus, his death on the cross (see Luke 9:31), marks the transformation of his prayer and the prayer of his people. Jesus died as he lived: praying, in a dialogue of filial intimacy with the Father. He died praying the psalms, specifically Psalm 22, which is the song of a righteous man who is beaten, his hands and feet pierced, his clothes divided, and his faith in God's deliverance mocked. In this final prayer, Jesus shows that he was "the true speaker of this psalm" and that the "Scripture became flesh in him, became the actual passion of this Righteous One [depicted in the psalm]: and that he thus inserted his death into the Word

25. See Mark 9:4.
26. *Jesus*, 306–7.
27. *Song*, 16.

of God, in which he lived and which lived in him, declaring itself in him."[28]

As we will discuss more completely below, Benedict sees an inherent unity between the prayer of Jesus on the cross and his words at the Last Supper. Hence Benedict sees a liturgical consummation to the New Testament's portrayal of Christ's mission: "He fashioned his death into an act of prayer, an act of worship"—a sacrificial offering of his whole self, his body and blood, to his Father.[29]

By turning his death into an act of prayer, a prayer that was accepted by God as evidenced in his resurrection, Jesus made it possible for all peoples "to participate in his most intimate and personal act of being, that is, his dialogue with the Father."[30] Our filial relationship with God becomes possible because on the cross Jesus shows himself to be the fulfillment of Israel's Scriptures and liturgy, thus revealing the God of Israel's fathers to be the God of the nations.[31]

The Church, therefore, is the renewed people of God, the "catholic" or universal family of God, opened to all so that they may embrace the God of Israel as their Father. This embrace of salvation can take place only if we insert ourselves into the prayer of Jesus. We do this by becoming one with him through our own prayer of love, our own act of surrendering our lives in prayer to God. This entrance into the prayer of Jesus begins in the filial affirmation of baptism, where we too are able in the Spirit to address God as our Father.[32] As we will see in the next chapter, our prayer reaches its zenith in the *oratio*, the Eucharistic Prayer of the Mass.

In the prayer of the Church, which is the prayer of Christ, we experience the ultimate intimacy of the dialogic character of revelation. "Praying actualizes and deepens our communion of being with God."[33] We can speak to God because God has spoken to us—because he has come to us as a Word and because in his inmost

28. *Pierced*, 23, 24.
29. *Pierced*, 22.
30. *Pierced*, 30.
31. See *Pierced*, 29: "This universalization of the tradition is its ultimate ratification, not its abrogation or replacement."
32. See Rom. 8:15–16; Gal. 4:6.
33. *Jesus*, 130.

life in the Trinity he is a relationship.[34] The prayer of Jesus reveals that the heart of the Trinity is a familial, filial relationship of love. God in his inner essence is a dialogue of love, and our prayer, both corporately in the liturgy and privately, is a participation in this filial and familial dialogue.[35]

The family prayer that Jesus taught his followers, the "Our Father," illuminates this point. Even when the believer prays the "Our Father" privately, he or she prays as a member of the family of God. It is never "*my*" Father. The prayer of Jesus is always personal and simultaneously the prayer of one who knows himself to be a part of a family. "Prayer is always praying *with* someone,"[36] in the communion of the Church, in the body of Christ, in the family of God.

As our prayer is never alone, neither is it something we can do of our own initiative. Prayer and worship are our response to the God who has first spoken to us. God's Word to us is a gift, the gift of himself; it is the opportunity to participate in his familial dialogue of love. This has two implications. First, it implies that our worship is never the work of the Church, never our own invention. "[Worship] is a response to an initiative coming from above, to a call and an act of love which is mystery."[37]

We can respond to God's words and deeds in prayer and worship because he calls us into the dialogue that he *is*. As Benedict says, God himself "is the content of Christian prayer."[38] In our prayer we ask for no less than the gift of God's self.[39] We have the audacity to ask for that gift because he has first given himself to us, in a most definitive way, on the cross. The prayer of the Church, the liturgy, becomes, then, a participation in Christ's work of self-giving. Liturgy is the "*opus Dei*, the work of God—God's action in us and with us."[40]

34. See *Faith*, 25–26: "It is only because God himself is the eternal dialogue of love that he can speak and be spoken to. Only because he himself is relationship can we relate to him"; see also 136.
35. *Liturgy*, 33.
36. *Faith*, 30.
37. *Song*, 119.
38. *Pilgrim*, 49.
39. *Faith*, 31.
40. *Song*, 118.

The New Passover and the Drama of the Last Supper

To understand Benedict's vision of this *opus Dei* and how it plays out in the divine liturgy of the Church, we must first look at his understanding of the crucifixion and the Last Supper. In his treatment of these subjects, Benedict uses the findings of historical and literary research to reconcile a long-noticed discrepancy between John's Gospel and the testimony of the other Gospel writers. This is not merely an academic exercise for Benedict. Rather, it helps him to penetrate the deeper meaning of the New Testament witness and hence the economy of salvation and the revelation of God.

The scholarly issue is this: All four Gospels agree that Jesus died on a Friday, several hours before sundown and the beginning of the Jewish Sabbath. According to John, however, Jesus was condemned to death at the moment when the Passover lambs were being slaughtered in the temple. If that is correct, then it means he died *before* Passover, which is contrary to the reports of the other Gospels, all of which maintain that Jesus celebrated the Passover meal with his apostles on the night before he died.[41]

Benedict adopts a solution suggested by study of the Dead Sea Scrolls. The scrolls indicate that the radical Essene sect at Qumran followed a 364-day *solar* calendar. By contrast, the priests and Sadducees in charge of the official temple cult followed a 354-day *lunar* calendar. For the Essenes, Passover would always be celebrated on a Tuesday night, while the official feasts were moveable, depending on the lunar calendar. Hence Benedict concludes that it is "a highly plausible hypothesis" that Jesus celebrated his last Passover meal according to the Essene calendar, on Tuesday night (which Jews would have considered early Wednesday), while according to the official calendar the meal would have been celebrated on Thursday night (early Friday).

This historical finding resolves the contradiction but does not exhaust the task of theological interpretation. Thus Benedict presses his exegetical conclusion into service of his spiritual and theological conclusion, namely, that John's account intends to depict Jesus as

41. Compare John 19:14 with Matt. 26:17–20; Mark 14:12–17; and Luke 22:7–16.

"the true Lamb" and the "living Temple" of the "new Passover"
accomplished by his death on the cross.

> Jesus truly shed his blood on the eve of Easter at the time of the
> immolation of the lambs. In all likelihood, however, he celebrated
> the Passover with his disciples in accordance with the Qumran
> calendar, hence, at least one day earlier; he celebrated it without
> a lamb, like the Qumran community which did not recognize
> Herod's temple and was waiting for the new Temple. Consequently,
> Jesus celebrated the Passover without a lamb—no, not without
> a lamb: instead of the lamb he gave himself, his Body and his
> Blood. . . .
>
> Jesus celebrated the Passover without a lamb and without a
> temple; yet, not without a lamb and not without a temple. He
> himself was the awaited Lamb, the true Lamb, just as John the
> Baptist had foretold at the beginning of Jesus' public ministry:
> "Behold, the Lamb of God, who takes away the sin of the world!"
> (John 1:29). And he himself was the true Temple, the living Temple
> where God dwells and where we can encounter God and worship
> him.
>
> His Blood, the love of the One who is both Son of God and true
> man, one of us, is the Blood that can save. His love, that love in
> which he gave himself freely for us, is what saves us. The nostalgic,
> in a certain sense, ineffectual gesture which was the sacrifice of an
> innocent and perfect lamb, found a response in the One who for
> our sake became at the same time Lamb and Temple. Thus, the
> cross was at the center of the new Passover of Jesus.[42]

This rich quotation, from a Holy Thursday homily, gives us a
taste of Benedict's preaching as pope. It also introduces the depth
of his theological considerations on the meaning of the cross
and its relationship to the Eucharist. The poverty of so much
theological and liturgical thinking today stems in part from the
inability of historical and literary exegesis to reckon with the
crucifixion. If it is true, as so many exegetes maintain, that Jesus
was simply an ordinary rabbi who did not claim to be God or
the Messiah, then the cross makes no sense. The reaction of Jew-

42. Pope Benedict XVI, Homily, Mass of the Lord's Supper (April 5, 2007).

ish and Roman authorities comes across as implausibly drastic and capricious. As Benedict observes: "People do not crucify the average professor."[43]

Here we see an instance of how the historical method's philosophical prejudices make it incapable of explaining the testimony of the texts. Presuming that a man cannot work miracles or credibly claim to be God, exegetes are at a loss to explain why this man was perceived to be a threat by both religious and civil authorities. For Benedict, the plain sense of the texts is the most reasonable sense, even apart from the claims of faith. The crucifixion, in fact, confirms what the New Testament tells us about Jesus' self-understanding and his words and deeds, namely, that he was in fact someone of quite extraordinary wisdom and power.[44] More directly important for our purposes is the fact that without an accurate understanding of the biblical data on the crucifixion, we cannot reach proper theological conclusions about the nature of Jesus' mission or the ministry of his Church.

In Benedict's biblical theology, the event of the cross is best understood according to the interpretation Jesus himself gives during the the Last Supper. This reading of Christ's death, which carries through all the New Testament writings, sees the cross in both cultic and salvation-historical terms. The cross is a liturgical-sacrificial act by which God is making a new covenant with humankind, fulfilling the expectations and inner meaning of Old Testament history.[45]

Benedict offers a careful examination of the texts by employing exegetical studies as well as the Church's patristic and liturgical tradition. As he reads them, Jesus' words at the Last Supper bring together Israel's covenantal history and sacrificial law, evoking the Old Testament festivals of Passover and the Day of Atonement. Benedict hears in Jesus' words quotations and deep echoes from the prophets and psalms, not to mention the Mosaic covenant at Sinai.

The climactic declarations—"this is my body . . . this is my blood"—come from Israel's cult. In offering his blood, Jesus alludes to a long history of the ritual shedding of blood, especially the blood

43. *Eschatology*, 28.
44. *Eucharist*, 28.
45. *Pilgrim*, 94–95, 97. *Religions*, 41; *Catechism*, 91–92, 96.

of the first Passover (Exod. 12:23) and the blood of the covenant at Sinai, to which he refers directly (Exod. 24:6, 8; Matt. 26:28).

Alluding to the covenant and temple sacrifices, Jesus describes the intent of his sacrifice with a further allusion to the prophet Isaiah, rendered in the Last Supper accounts variously as the blood "which is given for you" or "which is shed for you and for many" (Matt. 26:28; Mark 14:24; Luke 22:20). In these sayings, Jesus takes up the Old Testament figure of the righteous man who suffers for his faith in God. This theme runs through the psalms and gains great intensity in the sufferings of Job and in the prophet Daniel's account of the three men in Nebuchadnezzar's fiery furnace before reaching a nationalistic and messianic pitch in the so-called suffering servant songs of Isaiah.

Benedict sets Jesus' use of Isaiah in the context of Israel's national story. The servant songs (Isa. 53) reflect Israel's faith during its exile in Babylon, when its temple was destroyed and its worship was thereby rendered impossible. The calamity of the exile results in a profound national soul-searching over Israel's covenant relationship with God and the ways and means of worship and sacrifice.

The prophets, among others, came to the realization that the only authentic worship Israel could offer was "to suffer for the sake of its God." They also realized that because of the nation's sinfulness and guilt, Israel could never "play the part of the servant of God properly and completely." Benedict finds this recognition written between the lines of the servant songs as a kind of yearning expectation for one who was yet to come, the true servant, "the undefiled witness to God." In taking up Isaiah's words, then, Jesus identifies himself as that long-anticipated true witness, who in his blamelessness could offer himself to God for all humanity.[46]

Jesus' use of the expression "new covenant in my blood" (Luke 22:20; 1 Cor. 11:25) not only looks back to Moses and Sinai but also looks beyond the old covenant to Jeremiah's promise of a new one. This covenant would not be like the covenant made at Sinai (Jer. 31:31–34), and Benedict teases out the universal significance in

46. *Eucharist*, 33–34.

Jeremiah's prophecy. The new covenant Jeremiah foretells "will no longer be limited to physical descendants of Abraham, no longer to the strict keeping of the Law, but will spring from out of the new love of God that gives us a new heart."[47]

The Staggering Realism of the New Covenant

As radically new as it is, the new covenant's full significance nonetheless cannot be gauged except in light of the old covenant. Benedict's interpretation is again dependent on the wealth of scholarship on the covenant, scholarship to which we referred in the previous chapter. He sees in the upper room at Jerusalem a profound "spiritualization" of the Sinai event yet with the same essential purpose, namely, to seal a covenant by which a people are consecrated to God as his family, his "blood" kin.

As we discussed earlier, in sprinkling the sacrificial "blood of the covenant" on the altar and then on the people (Exod. 24:6, 8), Moses was evoking the ancient notion of covenant as forming a "blood association" between the covenant partners. In a literal and symbolic sense he was making Israel and God "brothers of the same blood."[48] When Jesus uses these same words at the Last Supper to refer to the cup, "*the words of Sinai are heightened to a staggering realism*, and at the same time we begin to see a totally unsuspected depth in them."[49]

What makes Jesus' words so staggeringly realistic is that unlike Moses he offers not a substitute, such as a fatted calf or lamb, in sacrifice but himself. The kinship made possible by Jesus' sacrifice is thus not "symbolic" or "representational," as in the case of Sinai; rather, it is *real*. It is "a blood brotherhood between God and man" effected by a true communion with God's own body and blood. What at Sinai was only "a hesitant attempt is here achieved. He who is the Son of God, he who is man, gives himself to the Father

47. *Eucharist*, 38.

48. *Religions*, 59–60. Benedict is here quoting the work of Gottfried Quell and Johannes Behm in "*Diatheke*," *Theological Dictionary of the New Testament*, ed. Gerhard Kittel, 10 vols. (Grand Rapids: Eerdmans, 1964), 2:104–34.

49. *Religions*, 60; emphasis added.

in dying and thus shows himself to be the one who *brings us all into the Father*. He now institutes true blood brotherhood, *a communion of God and man.*"[50]

What takes place here is both spiritualization *and* the greatest possible realism. For the sacramental blood fellowship that now becomes a possibility brings those who accept it into an utterly concrete—and corporeal—community with this incarnate human being, Jesus, and hence with his divine mystery. . . . The God who has come down thus draws man up into his own realm. Being related to God means a new and profoundly transformed level of existence for man.[51]

50. *Eucharist*, 38–39; emphasis added.
51. *Religions*, 60. See also, Pope Benedict XVI, Homily, Mass of the Lord's Supper (April 9, 2009):

After the bread, Jesus takes the chalice of wine. The Roman Canon describes the chalice which the Lord gives to his disciples as *praeclarus calix* (the glorious cup), thereby alluding to Psalm 23, the psalm which speaks of God as the Good Shepherd, the strong Shepherd. There we read these words: "You have prepared a banquet for me in the sight of my foes. . . . My cup is overflowing"— *calix praeclarus*. The Roman Canon interprets this passage from the Psalm as a prophecy that is fulfilled in the Eucharist: yes, the Lord does indeed prepare a banquet for us in the midst of the threats of this world, and he gives us the glorious chalice—the chalice of great joy, of the true feast, for which we all long—the chalice filled with the wine of his love. The chalice signifies the wedding-feast: now the "hour" has come to which the wedding-feast of Cana had mysteriously alluded. Yes indeed, the Eucharist is more than a meal, it is a wedding-feast. And this wedding is rooted in God's gift of himself even to death. In the words of Jesus at the Last Supper and in the Church's Canon, the solemn mystery of the wedding is concealed under the expression "novum Testamentum." This chalice is the New Testament—"the New Covenant in my blood," as Saint Paul presents the words of Jesus over the chalice . . . (1 Cor. 11:25). The Roman Canon adds: "of the new and everlasting covenant," in order to express the indissolubility of God's nuptial bond with humanity. The reason why older translations of the Bible do not say *covenant*, but *testament*, lies in the fact that this is no mere contract between two parties on the same level, but it brings into play the infinite distance between God and man. What we call the new and the ancient covenant is not an agreement between two equal parties, but simply the gift of God who bequeaths to us his love—himself. Certainly, through this gift of his love, he transcends all distance and makes us truly his "partners"—the nuptial mystery of love is accomplished. In order to understand profoundly what is taking place here, we must pay even greater attention to the words of the Bible and their original meaning. Scholars tell us that in those ancient times of which the histories of Israel's forefathers

We should pause here to take note of Benedict's theological hermeneutic at work. In his reading, the language and actions of the original Sinai covenant bear within them a fuller, spiritual significance intended by God. They point to the future new covenant to be made on the cross in the blood of Christ and to be represented and renewed in the eucharistic worship established at the Last Supper.

The symbolism of the covenant also is spiritualized, as a new people is born, not of blood or the will of the flesh, but of faith in the Son of God. "It is not blood kinship with the Lord that makes a person blessed—not flesh and blood, not race and descent, not blood and soil, not nation and class—but the spiritual kinship of faith."[52]

We also notice here that in Benedict's reading the canonical text of Scripture is shown to have a certain liturgical trajectory and teleology. All of salvation history was straining toward the cross, which can never be separated from the interpretation of the cross given at the Last Supper.[53]

At the Last Supper, Jesus announces the new and final covenant in biblical salvation history. This covenant does not abrogate the old covenant at Sinai but prolongs and renews it. The blood of the covenant is Christ's, given for the sake of the world. He himself is the new covenant by which "God binds himself irrevocably" to his creation.[54] As the covenant blood at Sinai symbolized the sharing

---

speak, to "ratify a covenant" means "to enter with others into a bond based on blood or to welcome the other into one's own covenant fellowship and thus to enter into a communion of mutual rights and obligations." In this way, a real, if non-material form of consanguinity is established. The partners become in some way "brothers of the same flesh and the same bones." The covenant brings about a fellowship that means peace. Can we now form at least an idea of what happened at the hour of the Last Supper, and what has been renewed ever since, whenever we celebrate the Eucharist? God, the living God, establishes a communion of peace with us, or to put it more strongly, he creates "consanguinity" between himself and us. Through the incarnation of Jesus, through the outpouring of his blood, we have been drawn into an utterly real consanguinity with Jesus and thus with God himself. The blood of Jesus is his love, in which divine life and human life have become one.

52. *Dogma*, 110.

53. Cf. Scott W. Hahn, "Worship in the Word: Toward a Liturgical Hermeneutic," *Letter & Spirit* 1 (2005): 101–36, esp. 130.

54. *Religions*, 62–65.

of flesh and blood between God and Israel, this new sharing is
universalized and made real—made literal—in the blood of Christ,
in which all nations come to worship the God of Israel and are
thereby made kin, flesh and blood, one body with Christ.

"A Body You Have Prepared for Me"

The cross, anticipated and interpreted by Jesus in his Last Supper
discourse, announces the transformation of sacrifice. In the history
of religion there has never been a sacrifice like that of Christ on
the cross. To make this assertion, Benedict's theology of the cross
and the Eucharist draws on anthropological and historical study
of religion, especially the study of ritual sacrifice.

Throughout history, as he understands it, sacrifice has been
based on a principle of symbolic representation or substitution.
Men and women offer in sacrifice something they value, for instance, the unblemished firstborn of their flock or the firstfruits
of their harvest. This offering is intended to symbolize or represent their own lives. In offering this valued good by destroying it
through a sacrificial fire or other means, the worshiper aims to
satisfy, propitiate, or secure some favor from the deity.

Benedict reads this anthropological data in light of the biblical
history of sacrifice. Although the God of Israel was truly unique
among the deities of the ancient Near East, Israel's system of sin
offerings was characterized primarily by this substitutionary principle. The blood and fat of the sacrificial animal symbolized and
was a substitute for the life of the one offering the sacrifice.[55]

This system, in Benedict's reading of the Bible, reflects the fallen
condition of man. Since the original sin and fall from grace, humankind has been closed in on itself. Men and women could not
offer themselves to God fully. They could never achieve the purity or
the communion with God for which they were intended. Made for
divinization in offering themselves and the fruits of creation back to
God in a free return of thanksgiving and love, men and women could
only offer sacrifices for forgiveness and atonement, for expiation and

55. *Pilgrim*, 76.

healing.[56] Over time, the canonical record indicates Israel's growing awareness of the hollowness and ineffectiveness of these efforts.

> All pre-Christian worship rests finally on the notion of representation. Man knows that he would basically have to give himself if he would honor God in a way suited to the deity. But he soon discovers the impossibility of giving himself and so creates the substitution: hecatombs of immolated victims are loaded on the altars of antiquity. A powerful cult is established but an oppressive futility pervades over all this, for there is nothing man can replace himself with. Whatever he offers remains too little.[57]

Long before the time of Christ, Israel, in dialogue with the wider Hellenistic culture, produced a critique of the notion of representational sacrifice. The system of ritual substitutional sacrifices came to be seen for what it truly is: an evasion, "a flight from reality, a flight from the call of God who wants us ourselves and who is truly worshipped in the gesture of unconditional love alone."[58] This recognition is reflected in Israel's psalms and prophets, where God is heard to complain with increasing frequency: "The world and all that is in it is mine. Do I eat the flesh of bulls or drink the blood of goats?" (Ps. 50:12–13).

Benedict detects in this development the influence of Hellenistic ideals of worship and Israel's own experience of exile and captivity. In particular, he points to the emerging idea of worship in the "word." This was the belief that through the expression of words, or prayer, the person might make an offering of his or her whole mind and heart to God. This belief is seen in the increasing sense in the prophets and the psalms that prayers of thanksgiving and praise, along with the interior dispositions of contrition and humility, are the true sacrifices acceptable and pleasing to God.[59]

---

56. *Liturgy*, 35–38.
57. Joseph Ratzinger, *The Sabbath of History* (Washington, DC: William G. Congdon Foundation, 2000), 27; Joseph Cardinal Ratzinger, *Introduction to Christianity*, trans. J. R. Foster (San Francisco: Ignatius, 1990 [1968]), 214–18.
58. Ratzinger, *Sabbath*, 27.
59. *Eucharist*, 48; *Liturgy*, 45–48; *Pilgrim*, 115; *Song*, 120. See also Ps. 50:8–14; 51:16–17; 69:30–31; 119:108.

As we will see in subsequent chapters, this idea of "verbal sacrifice"[60] influenced the notion of spiritual worship in the New Testament and is even reflected in the Eucharistic Prayer of the early Church. Indeed these ideals influenced the early Christian understanding not only of Christ's work on the cross but also of his entire work, beginning with his incarnation. "The dynamic of sacrifice is comprehended in the incarnation, on the basis of the psalms, the Letter to the Hebrews interpreted the process of incarnation as an actual dialogue within the Divinity: 'A body have you prepared for me,' says the Son to the Father (Heb. 10:5–7; Ps. 40:6–8). Thus, the entire Gospel is contained within this single statement."[61]

The cross, then, becomes the hermeneutical key for understanding the true nature of sacrifice and worship as well as the meaning of Christ's mission. By his cross, Jesus shattered forever the notion of representational or substitutionary sacrifices. In the cross, divine self-offering is made the pathway and the model for human worship of God. On the cross, a truly pure and innocent man offers himself—heart and mind, body and blood, soul and strength—for the love of God and obedience to the divine will.

In this, Christ's self-sacrifice corresponds to and brings to fulfillment "the inner drama" of the history of sacrifice found in the Old Testament.[62]

> What had always been intended and could never be achieved in the Old Testament sacrifices is incorporated in him. God does not desire the sacrifice of animals; everything belongs to him. And he does not desire human sacrifice, for he has created man for living. God desires something more: he desires love, which transforms man and through which he becomes capable of relating to God, giving himself up to God. Now, all those thousands of sacrifices that were always presented to God in the Temple at Jerusalem and all the sacrifices performed in the whole course of history, all this vain and eternal striving to bring ourselves up to God, can be seen as unnecessary

60. *Faith*, 37.
61. *Eucharist*, 14; see also 21.
62. *Liturgy*, 37.

and yet, at the same time, as being like windows that allow us, so to speak, a glimpse of the real thing, like preliminary attempts at what has now been achieved. What they signified—giving to God, union with God—comes to pass in Jesus Christ, in him who gives God nothing but himself and, thereby, us in him.[63]

The Lamb of Sacrifice in the History of Religion

It is crucial for Benedict's biblical theology that Christ's death be understood as the nascent Church understood it, namely, as a work of *sacrifice*. Such language has largely been abandoned in exegetical and theological circles today, in part because of researchers' prior assumptions that Jesus understood himself to be a kind of millennial rabbi, not the Son of God.[64] As Benedict reads the history, however, the early Church knew that Jesus' words at the Last Supper would have been "an empty gesture without the reality of the cross and the resurrection."[65]

The drama of the cross is inseparably bound as a single "paschal mystery" with the words, gestures, and promises of the Last Supper and the event of the resurrection. From the outside, from a strictly historical and literary perspective, the crucifixion is a gruesome episode of primitive capital punishment. But seen in the light of faith, it can be understood in its interior and spiritual depths, that

63. *Eucharist*, 32–33. See also Ratzinger, *Sabbath*, 28–29: "God dies as man. He gives himself entirely to men who are not wont to give themselves to him, and he thereby substitutes the reality of his all-sufficient love for the futile cultic substitution. The Letter to the Hebrews has further extended the brief allusion of John's Gospel and interpreted the Jewish liturgy of the Day of Atonement as an imaginative prelude to the real liturgy of the life and death of Jesus Christ. What was presented to the eyes of the world as a thoroughly profane event, as the execution of a man who was condemned as a political criminal was, in fact, the only real liturgy of world history. It is cosmic liturgy. . . . He does not offer the blood of substitute beings but rather his own—as is fitting, for true love can give nothing less than itself. . . . The Temple curtain is torn; from now on there is no worship any longer but the participation in the love of Jesus Christ, which is the perpetual cosmic day of atonement. And to be sure, the idea of an exchange has gained in Jesus Christ an unheard of new significance. God himself in Jesus Christ has taken our place and all of us live only from the mystery of this substitution."

64. See Benedict's discussion in *Benedict XVI*, 142–44.

65. *Benedict XVI*, 147. See also *Faith*, 60n1.

is, as "an act of worship rendered to God . . . a sacrifice of expiation, a saving act of the reconciling love of God made man."[66]

Yet full understanding of the paschal mystery requires more
than attending to the prior interpretation that Jesus gives it at the
Last Supper. It also means entering into a spiritual, typological,
liturgical reading of Israel's history. For Benedict, the history of Old
Testament sacrifice—and indeed "the whole history of religion"[67]—
culminates and is transformed in the cross of Christ.

Benedict notes the ancient Jewish tradition that the temple was
built at Moriah, the site where Abraham had been told to offer in
sacrifice his beloved son, Isaac (Gen. 22:2; 2 Chron. 3:1).[68] Benedict
focuses on one detail of that story: after the sacrifice is stayed by the
angel from heaven, Abraham finds a lamb or a ram caught in a nearby
thicket and sacrifices it to God in place of his son (Gen. 22:13).

For Benedict, this connects Abraham to the biblical beginnings of
sacrifice found in Abel's offering of the firstlings of his flock (Gen.
4:4). But he finds a still deeper meaning in the scene: Abraham's
sacrifice of the lamb looks ahead to the sacrifice of the true Lamb
who is to come. This is the fulfillment of the words of faith uttered
by Abraham, "God himself will provide . . ." (Gen. 22:8).

Benedict's reading is rich and prayerful. He draws from the
Church Fathers whom, as he notes, "simply could not put this
story down."[69] He also avails himself of the Church's ancient liturgical tradition. He is intrigued by the tradition of *risus pascha-
lis*, the Easter laughter, which is rooted in a symbolic reading of
the etymology of Isaac's name and a belief that Easter should be
celebrated with joyful laughter at having been saved from death.
And his reading leads to a deeply spiritual interpretation in which
Isaac is a sign of all who know the joy that God has provided the
Lamb and that we do not have to die.[70]

We must reluctantly forego an appreciation of the depth and
beauty of Benedict's reading to point out the fundamentals nec-

66. *Benedict XVI*, 147.
67. *Pilgrim*, 97.
68. *Pierced*, 115.
69. *Pierced*, 116.
70. See the discussion in *Pierced*, 114–21.

essary for understanding his broader biblical theology. Reading the Old Testament drama in the light of the cross, he sees the lamb given to Abraham on Moriah as the "first herald"[71] of the true Lamb, Jesus Christ, who will come and entangle himself in our humanity and history in order to become our sacrifice that frees us from death and reconciles us to God. "God . . . not only provides but provides himself in becoming the Lamb, so that man may become man and may live."[72]

Because he comes from God, the true Lamb is "not a replacement but a true representative."[73] And because the true Lamb allows himself to be bound and sacrificed, his sacrifice can deliver us and enable us to offer ourselves to God.[74] As a result, the paschal mystery resonates down through history. Because God himself is the offering we make to God, the worship found in the paschal mystery can be accessible and "present to all times . . . in its interior content."[75] And because of the great gift of his sacrifice, we can participate in the redemption he won for us. We are able to do what humankind has not been able to do since the beginning: offer worship that is pleasing and acceptable to God. In this we move closer to the Father's plan for creation.[76]

We close this chapter with a beautifully evocative passage in which Benedict explains how the cross and resurrection are the ultimate meaning, not simply of the Exodus and Passover, but of all salvation history.

> The resurrection is the reawakening of him who had first died on the cross; its "hour" is the Passover of the Jews, the remembrance of the leading of the House of Israel out of slavery.

71. *Eucharist*, 46.
72. *Pierced*, 117.
73. *Liturgy*, 38.
74. *Benedict XVI*, 147.
75. *Benedict XVI*, 147.
76. See *Liturgy*, 47: "Now the vicarious sacrifice of Jesus takes us up and leads us into that likeness with God, that transformation into love, which is the only true adoration. In virtue of Jesus' cross and resurrection, the Eucharist is the meeting point of all the lines that lead from the old covenant, indeed from the whole of man's religious history. Here at last is right worship, ever longed for and yet surpassing our powers: adoration 'in spirit and truth.'"

Jesus' cross and resurrection are seen by faith in the context of the inner meaning of the Passover, as the ultimate Passover in which what has always been meant by that is seen for the first time in its true light. All salvation history is gathered here, as it were, in the one point of this ultimate Passover that thus includes and interprets salvation history, just as it is itself interpreted and illumined by salvation history. For it is evident now that this whole history is likewise an exodus history: a history that begins with the call of Abraham to go out from his country—and this going-out-from has been, ever since, its characteristic movement. It attains its deepest significance in the Passover of Jesus Christ . . . in the radical love that became a total exodus from himself, a going-out-from-himself toward the other even to the radical delivery of himself to death so that it can be explained in the words: "I am going away and shall return" (John 14:28)—by going, I come. The "living opening through the curtain," as the epistle to the Hebrews explains the Lord's going-away on the cross (Heb. 10:20), reveals itself in this way as the true Exodus that is meant by all the exoduses of history. Thus we see how the theology of resurrection gathers all salvation history within itself and . . . in a very literal sense, it becomes a theology of existence, a theology of *ex-sistere*, of that exodus by which the human individual goes out from himself and through which alone he can find himself. In this movement of *ex-sistere*, faith and love are ultimately united— the deepest significance of each is that *Exi*, that call to transcend and sacrifice the *I* that is the basic law of the history of God's covenant with man and, *ipso facto*, the truly basic law of all human existence. . . .

God's action . . . implies, of necessity, that "is" that faith soon formulated explicitly: Jesus *is* Christ, God *is* man. Hence man's future means being one with God and so being one with mankind, which will be a single, final man in the manifold unity that is created by the Exodus of love. God "is" man—it is in this formula that the whole greatness of the Easter reality has first been fully apprehended and has become, from a passing point in history, its axis, which bears us all.[77]

77. *Principles*, 189–90.

This long and extraordinarily rich passage indicates the powerful heights to which Benedict's biblical theology is capable of soaring. For our purposes here, however, I will point out only a few salient points. First, Benedict presumes a unity of the scriptural Word, a unity that constitutes a "salvation history" at the same time that it enables texts from the Gospel of John and the Letter to the Hebrews to illuminate ancient Scriptures concerning the call of Abraham and the Exodus. All is interpreted in light of the revelation of divine love on the cross. His theological discussion includes consideration of the meaning of the Greek text and a concise yet creative meditation on the philosophical concept of "existence."

Second, Benedict's sweeping spiritual exegesis stands out, an exegesis that sees the Exodus to be the fundamental meaning of "the history of God's covenant with man," revealed in Christ's "exodus of love." As is typical, Benedict here presumes knowledge of an important strain of historical and literary exegesis on the exodus motif in Scripture.[78] But Benedict does not stop there; rather, through a theological hermeneutic of faith, he yolks these exegetical findings to the Church's confession of faith that Jesus is true God and true man.

Had we more space, we could explore how for Benedict "the Exodus, making a cultural break, with its death and regrowth, is a basic pattern of Christianity."[79] Again and again Benedict returns to the Exodus as a fundamental structure for the movement of the Christian life. It is in this dynamic movement from slavery to freedom and from death to life that we must understand his notion of Christian worship and sacrifice as an exodus from the exile of the self to the promised land of God. "All worship is now a participation in this 'Pasch' of Christ, in his 'passing over' from divine to human, from death to life, to the unity of God and man."[80]

---

78. On the exodus motif, see Hahn, "Worship in the Word," 122–24 and the current research summarized there in note 59.

79. *Truth*, 86; see also 199–200; Ratzinger, *Introduction to Christianity*, 219–20.

80. *Liturgy*, 34.

8

The Cosmic Liturgy

The Eucharistic Kingdom and the World as Temple

From His Pierced Body: The Liturgy of the New Covenant

For Benedict, the cross of Jesus Christ is the turning point in the history of human religion. On the cross, a new understanding of God and worship sprouts from the seeds of the ancient sacrifices and Scriptures of Israel.

For eons, men and women were estranged from God, unable to escape the thickets of their own selfishness, sin, and guilt that prevented them from giving themselves purely and wholly to God. Created in the gift of divine love, they were too proud to accept their dependence on God and wanted to live only for themselves, as if they were gods in their own right. Closed in on themselves in prisons of egotism, they were unable to return God's love. Their sacrifices took the form of pale and fearful substitutes, replacements for the love they could not freely give, vain attempts to achieve healing, purification, and atonement. Most of all, their sacrifices could not free them from the universal law of death.

The cross marks a new and unprecedented type of sacrifice. Here an innocent man gives up his own life that others might live.

He does not destroy something else and offer it to God in place of himself but rather allows himself to be crushed in infirmity and in full freedom offers his dying as a gift for all men. Because that innocent man is also God, this sacrifice is able to destroy death and to reach through all ages and be present at all times. The cross, says Benedict, "is an act of new creation, the restoration of creation to its true identity."[1]

In Christ and his cross, true worship is once again made possible—the worship for which humanity was made in the beginning; the worship that unites flesh and blood, body and soul, spirit and matter, heaven and earth. "Because he turned death into a proclamation of thanksgiving and love, he is now able to be present through all ages as the wellspring of life, and we can enter into him by praying with him."[2]

The crucifixion is presented in the Scriptures as a cosmic liturgy, an offering of prayer and sacrifice that unites heaven and earth. We enter into that cosmic liturgy by praying with Christ in the liturgy of his Church, which is the new people of God created from the body of Christ pierced on the cross. As we have seen, Benedict understands the cross in light of a panoply of convergent typological prefigurements, including most prominently Abraham's "sacrifice" of Isaac and the Passover sacrifice. In the typological strain we have already considered in the last chapter, Jesus is the priest and the unblemished firstling, the lamb of sacrifice, offering his blood in a day of atonement for the family of God that they might pass over from death to life. But there are other typologies at work in the New Testament accounts.

We must consider two of these if we are to correctly understand the climax of Benedict's biblical theology, namely, his treatment of the liturgy of the new covenant. The first is the typology of the soldier piercing Jesus' "side" as he hung dead on the cross. Benedict notices, as did the Fathers, that the word here, *pleura*, is also used in the Greek account of Eve's creation from the "side" of Adam (John 19:34; Gen. 2:21–22 LXX). For him this becomes,

1. *Liturgy*, 34. See also *Eucharist*, 42–43.
2. *Eucharist*, 49–50.

as it did for the Fathers, a sign of the Church's birth from the body of Christ.

Jesus is the new Adam. Like the first Adam, Jesus enters into "sleep" and a new humanity, a new people of God, is born from his side by the intent and action of God. The blood and water that flow from his pierced side are symbols of the baptismal waters and the blood of the Eucharist, "the foundational sacraments . . . which, for their part, form the actual content of the Church's identity as Church."[3]

Through these sacraments of blood and water, the people of God are connected in an intimate communion with one another in the body of Christ. Christ's body is also the new temple, which is the second typology we must consider in order to understand the liturgy of the new covenant. In symbolic language, the Gospels tell us that Jesus' death on the cross marks the destruction of the old temple in Jerusalem and all that it stands for, especially its cult of sacrifice. Jesus goes to his death at just the time when the Passover lambs are being slaughtered in the temple, and his death is accompanied by the mysterious tearing of the great veil in the sanctuary.

> The Temple is first of all the dwelling place of God, the place of his presence in the world. For this reason it is the place of gathering in which the covenant is effected ever anew. It is a place of God's encounter with his people, and the people also finds itself in it. The Temple is the place from which God's Word goes out, the site where the standard of his instruction is set up and becomes visible over a long distance. . . .
>
> The tearing of the Temple curtain at the moment of Jesus' death on the cross signified that this building had ceased to be the place of the encounter for God and humans in this world. From the moment of Jesus' death, his Body, which was given up for us, is the new and

3. Joseph Ratzinger, *The Sabbath of History* (Washington, DC: William G. Congdon Foundation, 2000), 32. See also *Eucharist*, 42–43: "The Lord's opened side is the source from which spring forth both the Church and the sacraments that build up the Church"; and Pope Benedict XVI, *Sacramentum Caritatis*, Post-Synodal Apostolic Exhortation on the Eucharist as the Source and Summit of the Church's Life and Mission (February 22, 2007), 14.

true temple. The external destruction of the stone Temple in the year 70 only makes visible for all of history what already happened in the death of Jesus.

The following psalm verse has now come into full force: "Sacrifice and offering you do not desire, but a body you prepared for me" (Ps. 40:6; Heb. 10:5). Ritual has now gained its new and final meaning: we glorify God by becoming one body with Christ, that is, a new spiritual existence in which he embraces us completely, with life and limb (see 1 Cor. 6:7).

We glorify God by letting ourselves be pulled into that act of love which was fulfilled on the cross. Glorification and covenant, worship and life become inseparably one. Jesus' hour, which lasts until the end of time, consists in his being on the cross and drawing us to himself (John 12:32) so that we may all become "one" with him (Gal. 3:28).[4]

Here we begin to grasp the breadth of what Benedict means when he describes the Church as *communio* and as the body of Christ. From this body, the blood and water of the sacraments are to flow to the ends of the earth, creating a new family and bringing all men and women into the kingdom of God. The Church exists, as we have already suggested, to bring about this *communio* encounter—the divinization of creation—through the divine service of the liturgy.[5] This is what the Church's creed professes, a belief that the communion of God and man is the end of the story.

For Benedict, the Church's sacramental liturgy—the new covenant's worship—is the goal and consummation of the biblical story and the history of salvation. If everything in Scripture is ordered to the covenant that God wants to make with his creation, then everything in the Church is ordered to proclaiming that new covenant and initiating people into it through the sacramental liturgy. The Church's mission, therefore, is liturgical; its identity and actions are defined by the Word revealed in history. The liturgy of the Church is the work of Jesus continuing in time, transforming history[6] and divinizing men and women by transforming them

4. *Song*, 167–68.
5. *Principles*, 254–55.
6. *Benedict XVI*, 142.

into "new creations," children of God, and partakers of divine nature.[7]

The Church's worship, then, is far more than a congregational gathering. It is an act of *priesthood*, which has always been the duty of the people of God. "Through the sacrifice of Christ and its acceptance in the resurrection, the entire cultic and sacerdotal heritage of the old covenant has been handed over to the Church. . . . Yes, the priesthood of the Church is a continuation and an acceptance of the Old Testament priesthood, which in this radically new and transformed state finds its true fulfillment."[8]

The essence of the priesthood of the Church is this adoration and glorification of God—"that the whole world may become a temple and a sacrifice pleasing to God, that in the end God may be all in all (1 Cor. 15:28)."[9] The eucharistic liturgy, or the Mass, becomes the centerpiece of the identity of the new people of God. The eucharistic words of Jesus form "the heart of the Church."[10] By those words, Jesus made a new covenant, fusing the covenant traditions at Sinai and the hopes of the prophets into a new people with a new worship and new temple, the body of the risen Christ.[11]

From eternity, this new people was foreseen emerging from the people of the old covenant. The economy of God is always one of unity and continuity, not rupture and disjunction. And in its new covenant relationship with God, the Church moves forward as the fulfillment of God's intentions in establishing Israel as the people of God. "The early Church did not set herself against Israel; rather, she believed herself, in all simplicity, to be Israel's rightful continuation."[12]

What is true of Israel and the Church is likewise true of their liturgies. The new covenant's worship does not replace or abrogate but rather purifies and perfects Israel's worship. The eucharistic

7. *Benedict XVI*, 149.
8. *Pilgrim*, 174.
9. *Benedict XVI*, 302–3.
10. *Eucharist*, 32.
11. *Communion*, 26–28.
12. *Pilgrim*, 271.

liturgy "places us in continuity with Israel and the whole of salvation history."[13] The Eucharist is revealed as the fulfillment of all
the liturgies of the old covenant. As Israel's liturgical worship was
ordered to remembrance, memorial, and "renewal of the covenant,"
so too is the Eucharist.[14]

Crucified Love and the Abyss of Death

Benedict's study of the origins and development of the Mass is
finely detailed, synthesizes a wealth of scholarship, and represents
an important contribution to liturgical theology.[15] While he per-
ceives essential continuities with Israel's Passover traditions and its
prayers of blessings, for him the Christian liturgy is built on something new and decisively different: the event of the resurrection.

The victory over death is what distinguishes the Christian liturgy
from Israel's and from all others. Death, in fact, is a persistent
subtheme in Benedict's writings and lends to them their unshake-
able seriousness. The questions of religion and the meaning of the
Bible are not academic curiosities for him. They strike to the core
of the human being. All religion, as he sees it, attempts to answer
the question of death, for only in the context of death is the urgent
question of the meaning of life seen with clarity.[16]

Benedict brings this out in his creative study of the theology of
the Lord's Day, which is the day of the resurrection and the day of
Christian worship.[17] The early Christian ideas about Sunday worship represent, again, "the spiritualization of the Old Testament."[18]
He observes the convergence of several tracks of Old Testament

13. Pope Benedict XVI, Homily, Eucharistic Celebration at Cologne-Marienfeld,
Germany (August 21, 2005), in *L'Osservatore Romano*, Weekly Edition in English
(August 24, 2005), 11–12.

14. *Religions*, 62–65. See also *Eucharist*, 48–49.

15. *Eucharist*, 56–73; *Faith*, 33–60, 66–67; see especially the discussion at *Faith*,
40–42 and 66–67.

16. Pope Benedict XVI, *Spe Salvi*, Encyclical Letter on Christian Hope (November
30, 2007), 6.

17. For his fullest treatment of the meaning of Sunday, see *Song*, 59–77; *Co-Workers*,
124–25, 333–34.

18. *Song*, 72.

expectation in early Christian writings about the Eucharist and the Lord's Day. First, the day of the resurrection was the first day of the week, which for the Jews was a sign of creation. Second, it was also the "third day," associated in the Old Testament with theophany, that is, the revelation of God and his covenant. Finally, in calling it the Lord's Day, the first disciples adopted a term the prophets employed to refer to the anticipated coming of the Lord's definitive revelation and judgment.

In Benedict's synthesis, then, the Eucharist is the feast of the new creation and the new covenant, the celebration of God's definitive entry into history and his conquest of death. And every Eucharist likewise looks forward to the final Sabbath of history, when all creation will be united in the cosmic liturgy giving glory to God. "Eucharist is ordered to eschatology . . . the liberation of the world and ourselves from death."[19]

Christian worship, then, is a festival of the resurrection, the triumphant celebration of divine love being stronger than death. This marks a stark contrast with the liturgy of Israel. With St. John Chrysostom, Benedict points out that the Passover liturgy never intended to save people from the power of death. In fact, the killing of the paschal lamb could never be more than a symbol. In other words, it was an act of hope for the coming of "One who could accomplish what the sacrifice of an animal was incapable of accomplishing."[20]

In Jesus, the victory over death sought by Israel—and all mankind—is accomplished. What makes the Christian liturgy unique is this victory over death, this belief that in the body and blood of Christ we share in his victory, that those who live from him will have a life that no death can take away. The entire dynamism of Christian life, beginning in the symbolism of baptism, reflects

19. *Faith*, 45, 65. See also *Liturgy*, 95; Benedict XVI, *Sacramentum Caritatis*, 37. In *Song*, 63 Cardinal Ratzinger writes: "The resurrection means that God has retained power in history, that he has not relinquished it to the laws of nature. It means that he has not become powerless in the world of matter and matter-determined life. It means that the law of all laws, *the universal law of death*, is not the world's final power after all and that it does not have the last word. The last one is and remains he who is also the first one" (emphasis added).

20. Pope Benedict XVI, Homily, Mass of the Lord's Supper (April 5, 2007).

this movement from death to life. In this we glimpse the mystery of the Divine *eros*, which Benedict made the subject of his first encyclical as pope:

> Unfortunately, from its very origins, mankind, seduced by the lies of the Evil One, rejected God's love in the illusion of a self-sufficiency that is impossible (see Gen. 3:1–7). Turning in on himself, Adam withdrew from that source of life who is God himself, and became the first of "those who through fear of death were subject to life-long bondage" (Heb. 2:15). God, however, did not give up. On the contrary, man's "no" was the decisive impulse that moved him to manifest his love in all of its redeeming strength.
>
> It is in the mystery of the Cross that the overwhelming power of the Heavenly Father's mercy is revealed in all of its fullness. In order to win back the love of his creature, he accepted to pay a very high price: the Blood of his only begotten Son. Death, which for the first Adam was an extreme sign of loneliness and powerlessness, was thus transformed in the supreme act of love and freedom of the new Adam. . . . On the Cross, God's *eros* for us is made manifest.[21]

The Christian liturgy, then, cannot be seen as merely an appropriation of Jewish traditions or the simple reenactment of Jesus' Last Supper. The Last Supper itself was anticipatory. "The Last Supper looks to the cross, where Jesus' words of self-offering will be fulfilled, and to the hope of the resurrection. Apart from them

---

21. Pope Benedict XVI, Message for Lent 2007 (November 21, 2006). See also Pope Benedict XVI, Angelus Address (February 17, 2008):"The entire structure of Christian life . . . consists essentially in paschal dynamism: from death to life." See also Pope Benedict XVI, *Deus Caritas Est*, Encyclical Letter on Christian Love (December 25, 2005), 12: "The real novelty of the New Testament lies not so much in new ideas as in the figure of Christ himself, who gives flesh and blood to these concepts—an unprecedented realism. In the Old Testament, the novelty of the Bible did not consist merely in abstract notions but in God's unpredictable and in some sense unprecedented activity. This divine activity now takes on dramatic form when, in Jesus Christ, it is God himself who goes in search of the 'stray sheep,' a suffering and lost humanity. . . . His death on the cross is the culmination of that turning of God against himself in which he gives himself in order to raise man up and save him. This is love in its most radical form. By contemplating the pierced side of Christ (see John 19:37), we can understand the starting-point of this Encyclical Letter: 'God is love' (1 John 4:8). It is there that this truth can be contemplated."

it would be incomplete and unreal. Again, this means that the form of the Last Supper is not complete in itself."[22]

The Eucharist is the new Passover of Jesus only when the promises of the Last Supper are made real by Jesus' suffering and rising. While the Eucharist fulfills the worship of Israel, there is also a radical newness about it, a renewal of history and of the whole cosmos.[23] The paschal mystery for Benedict is a new song of salvation. Or better, the paschal mystery means that Israel's liturgical songs must now be sung in a new christological key. The psalmist's cry—"Sing to the Lord a new song"—becomes a prophecy of the passage from the old to the new covenant.

Benedict locates a long-overlooked dimension of the Eucharist in Israel's *todah* psalms. These psalms accompanied a "thanksgiving sacrifice" offered by Israelites who had been delivered from suffering or some life-threatening situation.[24] The psalm that Jesus prayed on the cross, Psalm 22, is a *todah* psalm; indeed, Benedict remarks that all of the psalms that were first interpreted christologically in the early Church are *todah* psalms.[25]

There is a certain formula in the *todah*. The believer recounts in prayer his experience of desperation in the face of certain death; he recalls crying out to the Lord for help and deliverance and vowing to sing of God's goodness in the *qahal* if he is delivered. The *todah* psalm, accompanied by an offering of unleavened bread and sometimes wine, is the fulfillment of his vow, as the believer glorifies God for this great deed of mercy, singing with all the joy and thanksgiving of one who has been freed from death.

Read in light of "the inner unity" of the Old and New Testaments, Benedict sees a "close connection between *todah* sacrifice and Eucharist, *todah* spirituality and christology." The *todah* sacrifice is fulfilled in the paschal mystery, and Benedict notices a more-intense "prophetic" tenor to Jewish expectation concerning

22. *Faith*, 60n1.
23. Benedict XVI, *Sacramentum Caritatis*, 10.
24. *Faith*, 51–60. Benedict's discussion includes a long and appreciative review of the scholarship of Hartmut Gese, of which he says, "I feel that its importance cannot be overestimated" (*Faith*, 58).
25. For instance, Ps. 40:1–12; 51; 69.

the *todah*. "The *todah* of Jesus vindicates the rabbinic dictum: 'In the coming [Messianic] time, all sacrifices will cease except the *todah* sacrifice. This will never cease in all eternity. All [religious] song will cease too, but the songs of *todah* will never cease in all eternity.'"[26] For Benedict, the *todah* is fulfilled in the cross and resurrection of the Christ, Jesus.

But again, it is fulfilled in a way that could not have been anticipated within the ordinary framework of Jewish expectation. The deliverance brought about by the cross is a deliverance not from some life-threatening peril but from death itself. Indeed, Benedict suggests that like so much in the Jewish tradition, the *todah* was awaiting its completion in the cross and resurrection by which the deliverance of all men from death becomes a reality.

> Particularly in the *todah* psalms one finds a type of prayer that grew out of the faith of Israel; this prayer, deep down inside, was on the path into the newness of the New Covenant. . . . But the truly new, which had hitherto been merely awaited, happened only now, in the mystery of Jesus Christ. The "new song" praises his death and resurrection and hence proclaims God's new deed to the whole world: that he himself has descended into the anguish of the human state and into the pit of death; that he embraces all of us on the cross with his stretched-out arms and, as the Risen One, takes us up to the Father across the abyss of the infinite divide separating Creator and creature, which only crucified love can cross.[27]

The Performative Power of the Sacrament

In the unity of the Last Supper and the crucifixion, Benedict is able to articulate the true depth of Scripture as the saving Word of God, for the redemption of the cross is renewed in the Eucharistic Prayer, the *oratio*. At the heart of the prayer is the scriptural Word. In reality, the entire Mass is composed of words and prayers taken from the Scriptures. But in the high point of the Mass, the event

26. *Faith*, 58.
27. *Song*, 101.

of the Last Supper is remembered in dramatic detail; and with the repetition of Jesus' eucharistic words ("This is my body") the bread and wine are transformed into the body of Christ.[28] The power of the Word in the liturgy to bring about this transformation flows from the inner logic of the cross and its intimate connection with Jesus' words at the Last Supper.

> The indissoluble bond between the supper and the death of Jesus is . . . plain: his dying words fuse with his words at the supper, the reality of his death fuses with the reality of the supper. For the event of the supper consists in Jesus sharing his body and his blood, that is, his earthly existence; he gives and communicates himself. In other words, the event of the supper is an anticipation of death, the transformation of death into an act of love. Only in this context can we understand what John means by calling Jesus' death the glorification of God and the glorification of the Son (John 12:28; 17:21). Death, which by its very nature, is the end, the destruction of every communication, is changed by him into an act of self-communication; and this is man's redemption, for it signifies the triumph of love over death. We can put the same thing another way: death, which puts an end to words and to meaning, itself becomes a word, becomes the place where meaning communicates itself.[29]

By his death on the cross Jesus transformed death into a life-giving word. The gospel is the good news of "the death of death," the good news that love is stronger than death. This is more than new information for the believer. In the Eucharist, the Word of the cross becomes the Word of salvation for all who believe. Again, this belief flows from the nature of the divine speech-act.

> Christianity was not only "good news"—the communication of a hitherto unknown content. In our language we would say: the Christian message was not only "informative" but "performative."

28. In the liturgy, the scriptural word is truly "the Word of transformation, enabling us to participate in the 'hour' of Christ. . . . It is the Word of power which transforms the gifts of the earth in an entirely new way into God's gift of himself, and it draws us into this process of transformation" (Homily, Eucharistic Celebration at Cologne-Marienfeld, Germany [August 21, 2005]).

29. *Pierced*, 24–25.

That means: the Gospel is not merely a communication of things that can be known—it is one that makes things happen and is life-changing. The dark door of time, of the future, has been thrown open.[30]

God's Word is performative and transformative. This is the testimony of the normative theologians, the authors of sacred Scripture. On the first page of Scripture, we read of God speaking the world into existence. And throughout the Old Testament, God's Word is both speech and act.[31] Jesus' speech, too, was always sacramental, bringing into being the realities that his words signified. As God's Word created the heavens and the earth, so Jesus' words were able to heal the sick and raise the dead. "Jesus' proclamation was never mere preaching, mere words; it was 'sacramental,' in the sense that his words were and are inseparable from his 'I'—from his 'flesh.' His word opens up only in the context of the signs he performed, of his life and of his death."[32]

Jesus' word remains inseparable from his "I" in the liturgy. Through the structures of apostolic succession, priests are to stand *in persona Christi* and to speak with the authority and power of God in the liturgy.[33] This understanding of the priest's representation of Christ in the liturgy is related to another concept that is important in Benedict's writings, something he refers to as "a structural law of biblical faith . . . [that] God comes to men only through men."[34] This "law" is seen most clearly at the origins of the covenant. Abraham proclaimed his faithfulness to God's calling through his words and deeds, thus becoming the father of the covenant people Israel. At the dawn of the

---

30. Benedict XVI, *Spe Salvi*, 2.

31. "God reveals himself in history. He speaks to humankind, and the word he speaks has creative power. The Hebrew concept *dabar*, usually translated as 'word,' really conveys both the meaning of *word* and *act*. God says what he does and does what he says" (Pope Benedict XVI, Message to the Youth of the World on the Occasion of the 21st World Youth Day [April 9, 2006], in *L'Osservatore Romano*, Weekly Edition in English [March 1, 2006], 3).

32. *Catechism*, 50. See also *Benedict XVI*, 309.

33. *Pilgrim*, 184; see also 165–66.

34. Joseph Ratzinger, *Faith and the Future* (Chicago: Franciscan Herald, 1971 [1970]), 34.

new covenant, God again comes to his people through a person, Mary.[35]

In the liturgy, God comes to us through the priest who becomes the voice of the divine Word.[36] The priestly word is the word of faith and the sacramental word of Christ. "As Christians we believe in the Word that has become flesh. . . . What has become visible in the Word has been transformed into the sacrament, as St. Leo the Great once said. The words of faith are essentially sacramental words."[37]

The Word in Worship: The Past Deeds of God Made Present

Scripture is central to the eucharistic celebration because the liturgy actualizes and continues the story of salvation that begins in the pages of the Bible. Indeed, Benedict is always aware that the Scriptures themselves have emerged from the context of the Church's liturgical worship. As he notes, cultic worship is "the intimate, vital atmosphere of the Bible, in both the Old and New Testament."[38]

The inner logic of Christian worship derives from the story of the disciples on the road to Emmaus (Luke 24:25–31). Benedict comes back to this story again and again in his teachings on the Eucharist.

> This marvelous Gospel text already contains the structure of Holy Mass: in the first part, listening to the Word through the Sacred Scriptures; in the second part, the Eucharistic liturgy and communion with Christ present in the Sacrament of his Body and his Blood. In nourishing herself at this two-fold table, the Church is constantly built up and renewed from day to day in faith, hope and charity.[39]

35. See *Eucharist*, 13: "For without Mary the entire process of God's stepping into history would fail of its object, would fail to achieve that very thing which is central in the Creed—that God is a God with us and not just a God in himself and for himself."

36. Unfortunately, we do not have the space here to develop Benedict's rich biblical, ecclesial, and christological understanding of the priesthood. For a good introduction to his thought, see *Benedict XVI*, 293–324.

37. *Song*, 174.

38. *Communion*, 15.

39. Pope Benedict XVI, Regina Caeli Address (April 6, 2008); General Audience (March 26, 2008). See also *Faith*, 47: "First we have the searching of the Scriptures,

The Liturgy of the Word in the Mass presumes the unity of salvation history and in fact tracks and unfolds that history, beginning with readings from the Law and the prophets, a song from the psalms, and then readings from the Gospels and the apostolic writings.[40] Yet it is a mistake to regard the Scriptures used in the liturgy as historical readings or even ethical lessons. They are the Word of God, the voice of revelation that speaks to us in the present with creative and life-changing power. Benedict remembers the stories of the saints, such as Anthony and St. Francis of Assisi, whose lives were totally changed by the Word they heard in the liturgy, touched, as it were, by the Word of the Lord.[41]

Even if the Word rarely produces such dramatic conversion experiences, it is always intended to be transformative. During the course of the liturgical year, the lectionary or plan of weekly Mass readings "enables man to go through the whole history of salvation in step with the rhythm of creation."[42] Through the Word read and prayed in the liturgy, the believer is slowly fashioned into the person God intends him or her to be.[43]

As we have noted, the Church reads the Scriptures typologically in its liturgy. This typological reading tends toward mystagogy, toward bringing about a kind of communion with the events proclaimed in the sacred pages. What Benedict has written in connection with early Christian liturgical art seems all the more applicable to the function of Scripture in the Christian liturgy:

---

explained and made present by the risen Lord; their minds enlightened, the disciples are moved to invite the Lord to stay with them, and he responds by breaking the bread for his disciples, giving them his presence and then withdrawing again, sending them out as his messengers." See also *Pilgrim*, 293–94.

40. *Eucharist*, 63; *Pilgrim*, 271.

41. Pope Benedict XVI, Address, Feast of the Presentation of the Lord (February 2, 2008).

42. *Co-Workers*, 2.

43. What Benedict says about the language of prayer applies well to his thoughts on the Liturgy of the Word: "The language of our Mother [the Church] becomes ours; we learn to speak it along with her, so that gradually, her words on our lips become our words. We are given an anticipatory share in the Church's perennial dialogue of love with him who desired to be one flesh with her" (*Faith*, 30).

On liturgical feasts the deeds of God in the past are made present. The feasts are a participation in God's action in time. . . . The individual events are now ordered toward the Christian sacraments and to Christ himself. Noah's ark and the crossing of the Red Sea now point to baptism. The sacrifice of Isaac and the meal of the three angels with Abraham speak of Christ's sacrifice and the Eucharist. Shining through the rescue of the three young men from the fiery furnace and of Daniel from the lions' den we see Christ's resurrection and our own. . . .

The point of the images is not to tell a story about something in the past, but to incorporate the events of history into the sacrament. . . . We are taken into the events. . . . The centering of all history in Christ is both the liturgical transmission of that history and the expression of a new experience of time, in which past, present, and future make contact, because they have been inserted into the presence of the risen Lord.[44]

As we can see, Benedict notices how the New Testament's typological interpretation of the Old is ordered to the sacramental encounter with Christ. We see in this passage, too, his sense of the mystery of the Word as living and active, bringing about the very promises that it speaks of in the life of the believer.

The Prayer of the *Logos* and the Spiritual Sacrifice

The sacred Word heard in the Mass and the sacrificial offering of that Word on the cross come together in what is known as the Canon, or the Eucharistic Prayer of the Church. In the Eucharistic Prayer of the Mass, we have the culmination of the creative power of God's Word in history.

For the Church Fathers, this prayer was the essence of the eucharistic liturgy. Some would refer to the Mass simply as the *oratio*, or prayer. For Benedict, too, the *oratio* has a certain summary quality, as it brings the mystery of God's salvific plan to a zenith.

The *oratio*, as we have introduced it, retells the story of salvation history, uniting the Old and the New Testaments. The climax of

44. *Liturgy*, 117.

this story—in both the prayer and the Scriptures—is the Last Supper and Jesus' words: "This is my body." Benedict acknowledges both Hebrew and Hellenistic influences on the *oratio*. It clearly reflects deep affinities and continuities with the Passover Haggadah and the prayer of blessing, the *Berakah*.[45] But in an important and unique observation, he also stresses the influence of "the mature religion of the Hellenistic world," in particular, the concept of "verbal sacrifice" (*logikē tysia*) found in late antiquity.[46]

We introduced this Hellenistic development in our discussion of the transformation of sacrifice in the previous chapter. For Benedict, this development is crucial for understanding the prayer of the Eucharist and how that prayer fulfills the divine intention for creation and salvation history. He sees the concept of the sacrificial word—mediated by the late Hebrew notion of the "sacrifice of praise" and St. Paul's call for "spiritual worship" (*logikē latreia*, Rom. 12:1)—in the Canon's petition for the Father to accept our *oblatio rationabilis*, which can be literally translated "rational sacrifice."

As Benedict interprets it, our "rational oblation" might be compared to a vow in which we give our "word," signifying ourselves, our entire beings. In the Eucharistic Prayer, we join our word of sacrifice—our offering of our whole hearts and minds—to the self-offering of the Word, the *Logos*, who became flesh in order to offer himself, flesh and blood, to the Father. "The Eucharistic Prayer is an entering-in to the prayer of Jesus Christ himself; hence it is the Church's entering-in to the *Logos*, the Father's Word, into the *Logos*' self-surrender to the Father, which, in the cross, has also become the surrender of mankind to him."[47]

We ask by this petition that we might be conformed ever more readily to the *Logos*.

> We ask that the *Logos*, Christ, who *is* the true sacrifice, may himself draw us into his act of sacrifice, may "logify" us, make us "more consistent with the Word," "more truly rational," so that his sac-

45. *Eucharist*, 49–50.
46. *Eucharist*, 51. See also *Faith*, 37.
47. *Faith*, 37. See also *Pilgrim*, 115; *Song*, 120.

rifice may become ours and may be accepted by God as ours, may be able to be accounted as ours. . . . We are asking . . . that we ourselves might become a Eucharist with Christ and, thus, become acceptable and pleasing to God.[48]

In this spiritual worship, this sacrifice consisting in words of prayer, we experience the final purification of sacrifice brought about by the cross. Through this prayer our lives become eucharistic and we experience "the transformation of existence into thanksgiving."[49]

> Sacrifice consists then—we shall say it once more—in a process of transformation, in the conformity of man to God, in his *theiosis*, as the Fathers would say. It consists, to express it in modern phraseology, in the abolition of difference—in the union between God and man, between God and creation: "God all in all" (1 Cor. 15:28). . . .
>
> The Greek thinkers had already [considered sacrifice] in relation to the Logos, to the Word itself, indicating that the sacrifice of prayer should not be mere speech but the transmutation of our being into the Logos, the union of ourselves with it. Divine worship implies that we ourselves have become beings of the Word, that we conform ourselves to the creative Intellect. But once more it is clear that we cannot do this of ourselves, and thus everything seems to end again in futility—until the day when the Word comes, the true, the Son, when he becomes flesh and draws us to himself in the exodus of the cross. This true sacrifice, which transforms us all into sacrifice, that is to say, unites us to God, makes of us beings conformed to God, is indeed fixed and founded on an historical event, but is not situated as a thing in the past behind us—on the contrary, it becomes contemporary and accessible to us in the community of the believing and praying Church, in its sacrament: *that is what is meant by the "sacrifice of the Mass."*[50]

48. *Pilgrim*, 116–17. Benedict adds that the Eucharistic Prayer reflects the New Testament ideal of worship: "I am persuaded that the Roman Canon has in its petition hit upon the real intention of Paul in his exhortation in Romans 12."

49. *Eucharist*, 48. See also *Eucharist*, 51; Benedict XVI, *Sacramentum Caritatis*, 64, 70; *Faith*, 70.

50. *Benedict XVI*, 149, 152–53; emphasis added.

Benedict's vision here is breathtaking, for he sees in Christian worship the fulfillment of the history of religion. We see here how, in the pierced side of Christ, the new Adam became a life-giving Spirit, the fruits of his saving work flowing to the ends of the earth through the sacraments of the Church.[51] Anticipating our discussion below, we see how in the Eucharist we take part in the festival of the world's redemption. We are inserted into the divine plan for human history and "incorporated into the great historical process by which the world moves toward the fulfillment of God being 'all in all.'"[52]

Before we turn to the cosmic liturgy, let us conclude our reflection on the Eucharistic Prayer. In this long passage, notice how easily Benedict integrates modern rhetorical insights into Scripture, especially speech-act theories, with the perspectives of liturgical theology and metaphysics in order to articulate a compelling, biblically grounded understanding of what truly happens in the divine liturgy:

> This *oratio*—the Eucharistic Prayer, the "Canon" is really more than speech; it is *actio* in the highest sense of the word. For what happens in it is that the human *actio* . . . steps back and makes way for the *actio divina*, the action of God. In this *oratio*, the priest speaks with the *I* of the Lord—"This is my body," "This is my blood." . . . This action of God, which takes place through human speech, is the real "action" for which all of creation is an expectation. The elements of the earth are transubstantiated, pulled, so to speak, from their creaturely anchorage, grasped at the deepest ground of their being, and changed into the body and blood of the Lord. The new heaven and new earth are anticipated. . . .
>
> This is what is new and distinctive about the Christian liturgy: God himself . . . inaugurates the new creation, makes himself accessible to us, so that, through the things of the earth, through our gifts, we can communicate with him in a personal way. . . . Precisely because God himself has become man, become body . . . he comes through his body to us who live in the body. The whole event of the incarnation, cross, resurrection, and second coming is present as the way by which God draws man into cooperation with

51. *Way*, 125, 126.
52. *Liturgy*, 59. See also *Liturgy*, 70–71, 103; *Benedict XVI*, 153–54.

himself. . . . True, the sacrifice of the *Logos* is accepted already and forever. But we must still pray for it to become *our* sacrifice, that we ourselves . . . may be transformed into the *Logos*, conformed to the *Logos*, and so made the true body of Christ.[53]

With these observations, we have reached the summit of the liturgy and the summit of Benedict's biblical theology. In the liturgy, we are drawn into contact with the very means of salvation history, the saving act of Christ on the cross. In the liturgy, the desire of God's condescension meets the desire of the human person for transcendence. The Eucharist we share becomes the bread of life on the basis of a profound "sacramental 'mysticism' grounded in God's condescension towards us."[54]

Anticipated *Parousia* and God "All in All"

In Benedict's biblical theology, liturgy is the goal of creation and of the human person. In the liturgy, the purposes of salvation history are realized—heaven and earth are filled with God's glory and each participant is swept up into the embrace of salvation, into the communion of God's eternal love. The communion God has desired since before the foundation of the world—between heaven and earth, between the visible and invisible, between the divine and human—is revealed and effected in the liturgy. The Church has been given a cosmic sacerdotal commission. "The ultimate end of all New Testament liturgy and of all priestly ministry is to make the world as a whole a temple and a sacrificial offering for God. This is to bring about the inclusion of the whole world into the Body of Christ, so that God may be all in all (1 Cor. 15:28)."[55]

Benedict's focus on the cosmic liturgy comes, once again, from taking seriously the witness of the New Testament authors. We

---

53. *Liturgy*, 172–74. It is unfortunately beyond my purposes here to address how this divine Word spoken by the ordained priest is efficacious. For what I would suggest are fruitful avenues for prayer and reflection on this topic, see *Faith*, 94 and *Eucharist*, 51.

54. Benedict XVI, *Deus Caritas Est*, 13.

55. *Communion*, 127–28.

have already noticed that the crucifixion is depicted as "a cosmic liturgy, as tearing open the closed-up heavens."[56] The full revelation of this liturgy and its connection to the eucharistic liturgy on earth is, of course, found in the book of Revelation, which in many ways reflects a spiritual interpretation of Christ's sacrifice on the cross.[57] Revelation reveals a cosmic liturgy, a liturgy of eternity. Every celebration of the Eucharist on earth, then, becomes an entering into the heavenly liturgy of eternity. "It is entering into the liturgy of the heavens that has always been taking place. Earthly liturgy is liturgy because and only because it joins what is already in process, the greater reality."[58]

In the liturgy, the eschatological orientation of Scripture is actualized. "In the celebration of the liturgy, the Church moves toward the Lord; liturgy is virtually this act of approaching his coming. In the liturgy the Lord is already anticipating his promised coming. Liturgy is anticipated *parousia*."[59]

This sense of the cosmic dimension has largely been lost in the modern period, another casualty of the philosophical flaws and overreaching of the historical-critical method. Benedict observes that in the modern period there arose a fundamental misunderstanding about the nature of liturgy and the Church, due in large part to faulty exegetical conclusions. Indeed, the *parousia*, the return or presence of Christ, and the general character of New Testament eschatological expectation have been sharply debated in modern biblical scholarship. For much of the last century, it has been an exegetical commonplace that the oldest New Testament writings are shot through with expectation of the imminent end of the world and the return of Christ, leading many scholars to conclude that "in his ideas about time Jesus was mistaken . . . [and] that Jesus' message is intrinsically incapable of being appropriated by us."[60]

56. *Pilgrim*, 93–94.
57. See *Pilgrim*, 110–11.
58. *Liturgy*, 70. See also *Song*, 130, 135, 175.
59. *Song*, 129.
60. *Eschatology*, 271. On parousia (translated "coming" in Matt. 24:27 and "presence" in 2 Cor. 10:10 and Phil. 2:12), see Scott Hahn, *Letter and Spirit: From Written Text to Living Word in the Liturgy* (New York: Doubleday, 2006), 104–21.

I do not have the space here to rehearse Benedict's thorough critique of this crucial exegetical mistake, but at work he sees many of the fallacious philosophical presumptions we discussed earlier when considering his critique of criticism. The chief deficiency is the methodological decision to consider the texts apart from the liturgy and the tradition of the Church. This has caused exegetes to ignore or downplay the fact that eschatological expressions like *parousia* and *maranatha* properly "belong in the context of early Christian eucharistic celebration."[61]

Benedict builds his argument on solid philological and historical grounds. He even brings in comparative religious and cultural data concerning the imperial liturgy of the Roman state and traditions of emperor worship in the ancient Near East. He agrees that the normative theologians who authored the New Testament expected a second coming or parousia of Christ. But, he adds, it is clear from the language and the contexts of the various texts that this coming and presence was anticipated, and in some way experienced, in every celebration of the Eucharist.

> The cosmic imagery of the New Testament cannot be used as a source for the description of a future chain of cosmic events. All attempts of this kind are misplaced. Instead, these texts form part of a description of the mystery of the *parousia* in the language of liturgical tradition. The New Testament conceals and reveals the unspeakable coming of Christ, using language borrowed from that sphere which is graciously enabled to express in this world the point of contact with God. The *parousia* is the highest intensification and fulfillment of the liturgy. And the liturgy is *parousia*, a *parousia*-like event taking place in our midst. . . . Every Eucharist is *parousia*, the Lord's coming, and yet the Eucharist is even more truly the tensed yearning that he would reveal his hidden glory. . . . In touching the risen Jesus, the Church makes contact with the *parousia* of the Lord.[62]

61. *Eschatology*, 6; see also 202–3. For Benedict's critique, see *Eschatology*, 35–45, 271–72. For the Aramaic expression *maranatha* ("Our Lord, come!"), see 1 Cor. 16:22; Rev. 22:20.
62. *Eschatology*, 202–4.

The eucharistic liturgy is our movement toward the Lord, who comes to meet us. Our worship is the worship of a people making their exodus from this world to the next, from history into eternity, in a "pilgrimage toward the transfiguration of the world."[63] This again is a dimension of our life in the eucharistic kingdom, in which we are to live in prayer for the coming of the kingdom, the kingdom that has already come in the person of Jesus. "Well then, the Church is that portion of humanity in whom Christ's royalty is already manifest, who has peace as its privileged manifestation. It is the new Jerusalem, still imperfect because it is yet a pilgrim in history, but able to anticipate in some way the heavenly Jerusalem."[64]

The Eucharist on earth is the liturgy, the song of a royal and priestly people on their pilgrimage. In the Eucharist the kingdom here on earth is in some measure realized and the final descent of the kingdom of heaven is anticipated. Thus Benedict can speak of participation in the Eucharist as "the royal privilege of the Christian."[65] The Eucharist is the food of the pilgrim people, just as God gave daily bread or manna to Israel in its pilgrimage toward the promised land.

In his interpretation of the Lord's Prayer, Benedict focuses on the mysterious Greek word *epioúsios*, translated "daily." He reminds us that the word is not found anywhere else in Greek literature until its use in the Gospels. Following the traditional patristic interpretation, he sees in this word a reference to the Eucharist and an allusion to the manna in the wilderness. He also finds it significant that the appeal for daily bread follows the appeal for the coming of the kingdom.

In fact, only the Eucharist can answer the question of what this mysterious word *epioúsios* means: the bread of the world to come, which is already given to us today, so that the world that is to

63. *Liturgy*, 49–50. See also *Song*, 121.
64. Pope Benedict XVI, Homily, Eucharistic Concelebration with the New Cardinals and Presentation of the Cardinal's Ring (November 25, 2007).
65. *Eucharist*, 103. See also Benedict XVI, *Sacramentum Caritatis*, 31: "Every eucharistic celebration sacramentally accomplishes the eschatological gathering of the People of God. For us, the eucharistic banquet is a real foretaste of the final banquet foretold by the prophets (see Isa. 25:6–9) and described in the New Testament as 'the marriage-feast of the Lamb' (Rev. 19:7–9), to be celebrated in the joy of the communion of saints"; *Way*, 111.

come might begin already in our midst today. And so, through this petition, the prayer that God's kingdom will come and earth will become like heaven becomes quite practical: through the Eucharist heaven comes to earth . . . God's tomorrow comes closer to us, so that his kingdom begins even today among us.[66]

In this pilgrimage, the hope of human history is seen stretching toward its final goal. The transformation that takes place at the altar can be seen as a "type," or prefigurement, of the eschatological transubstantiation of heaven and earth. This unspeakably beautiful vision is what the New Testament writers were trying to communicate with images such as the new Jerusalem, the new paradise, the heavenly bride. The world "must be conformed to the Eucharist."[67] It must become a new creation, in which God will be all in all.

This is the meaning of the early liturgical prayer, *Maranatha*.

The essence of the liturgy is finally summarized in the prayer that St. Paul (1 Cor. 16:22) and the *Didache* (10.6) have handed down to us: *Maran atha*—"our Lord is there—Lord, come!" From now on, the parousia is accomplished in the liturgy, but that is so precisely because it teaches us to cry: "Come, Lord Jesus," while reaching out toward the Lord who is coming. It always brings us to hear his reply yet again and to experience its truth: "Yes, I am coming soon" (Rev. 22:17, 20).[68]

All liturgy, then, is a liturgy of hope. A confident hope based on the fulfillment of all God's covenant promises throughout salvation history. An expectant hope, the hope of one who in joy awaits the fulfillment of the new covenant in "one Kingdom of God, in which there will be no further division because God will be all in all."[69] The hope of the one who knows that his Redeemer lives and is coming soon, and that when he does he will "finally hand over to the Father the Kingdom—that is, ingathered humanity and the creation that is carried with them (1 Cor. 15:28)."[70]

66. *Way*, 105.
67. *Benedict XVI*, 84.
68. *Benedict XVI*, 154.
69. *Co-Workers*, 29–30.
70. *Eucharist*, 145.

9

The Authority of Mystery

The Beauty and Necessity of the Theologian's Task

The Scripture Experts and the Simplicity of God

Benedict's biblical theology is a thing of great beauty and power. It reveals a man of striking erudition but also a man of deep prayer. In his exploration of the grand themes of creation, salvation history, and eternal life, he opens before us bright avenues of possibility for the study of sacred Scripture. Even more so, his hermeneutic of faith shows us new potentials for the practice of theology.

Benedict's synthesis promises a way of reading Scripture authentically. In other words, it promises a way of reading Scripture as it was written, that is, as a divine, living Word spoken in history to the Church, a Word whose meaning is understood within the broad unity of the Church's experience of the faith. This experience includes liturgy and dogma and is not limited to the expectations and contexts of a text's original audience. Benedict's approach marries prayer and research, science and spirituality in faith's search to understand the mystery of creation and the Lord of history.

In the previous pages, we have shown Benedict to be a true reformer in the spirit of authentic renewal. True development

and renewal in the Church, he has written, must always proceed
by a hermeneutic of continuity[1] and in the spirit of faithful reflection on the origins and sources of the Church, namely, the
Scriptures, the liturgy, the creeds, and the councils. In seeking
normative principles in the experience of the early Church and
in seeking new ways to express the truths of the faith, Benedict
is preparing the future for theologians and exegetes, as well as
for the Church.

For Benedict, exegetes and theologians must be people of faith,
men and women seeking to understand the mystery they have given
their lives to in the Church. Theology, as he conceives it, ultimately
can be nothing other than a form of service to the Church's mission
of spreading the gospel and gathering the eucharistic kingdom of
God. But even the secular academy, he has suggested, should be
able to make room for the faithful study of Scripture and theology
as part of its overall commitment to the search for truth. Benedict
once made a very insightful observation about the origin of Plato's
Academy. He noted that the rhythm of the academic life of the
Academy included cultic veneration and the offering of sacrifices.
"For Plato, who was the first to express it philosophically, the freedom of the truth belongs not merely accidentally but essentially
in the context of worship, of cult."[2]

This original sense of academic study as a dimension of worship and adoration needs to be recovered. As Benedict has pointed
out, it was the scholars and the scribes, the great exegetes of the
day, who were unable to recognize Jesus as the Christ. It is hard
not to hear a contemporary application in Benedict's reading of
Jesus' experience:

> It is not the Scripture experts, those who are professionally con-
> cerned with God, who recognize him; they are too caught up in
> the intricacies of their detailed knowledge. Their great learning
> distracts them from simply gazing upon the whole, upon the real-
> ity of God as he reveals himself—for people who know so much

1. Pope Benedict XVI, Address to the Roman Curia Offering Them His Christmas
Greetings (December 22, 2005).
2. *Theology*, 40–41.

about the complexity of the issues, it seems that it just cannot be so simple.[3]

At the Synod of Bishops in 2008, he recalled St. Augustine's meditation on the scribes and Pharisees consulted by Herod when the Magi arrived. As Augustine observed, they knew from their specialist knowledge of the Scriptures where the Savior was to be born, but they could not recognize the Savior himself. This is the danger for the scholar, as Benedict went on to explain:

> Just reading it does not mean necessarily that we have truly understood the Word of God. The danger is that we only see the human words and do not find the true actor within, the Holy Spirit. We do not find the Word in the words. . . . We stop at the human words, words form the past, history of the past, and we do not discover the present in the past, the Holy Spirit who speaks to us today in the words from the past. In this way we do not enter the interior movement of the Word, which in human words conceals and which opens the divine words. . . . We must always look for the Word within the words.[4]

We must keep looking for the Word within the words. This is essential for our own lives as believers.

It is also essential that we not unwittingly become an ally of the enemy. Benedict sometimes points with cautionary irony to Vladimir Soloviev's "A Short Story about the Anti-Christ." In the story, the Antichrist is a renowned exegete, so highly regarded that he is awarded an honorary degree in theology from the University of Tübingen. Benedict associates this story with New Testament traditions about the "antichrists" and with Jesus' temptation in the wilderness, where at one point the devil quotes and interprets a passage of Scripture. The point is that scholarship can, intentionally or not, end up denying the foundational assertion of the Church that Jesus is the *Christ*. "The fact is that scriptural exegesis can become a tool of the Antichrist. Soloviev is not the first person to tell us that; it is the deeper point of the temptation story itself. The alleged findings

3. *Jesus*, 342.
4. Pope Benedict XVI, Meditation during the First General Congregation of the Twelfth Ordinary General Assembly of the Synod of Bishops (October 6, 2008).

of scholarly exegesis have been used to put together most dreadful books that destroy the figure of Jesus and dismantle the faith."[5]

Lectio Divina, Humility, and a Truly Ecclesial Theology

What is needed is prayer and humility, the attitude that is always prerequisite to true prayer. Benedict finds the self-imposed anonymity of the sixth-century theologian Pseudo-Dionysius to be an eloquent lesson for theological and exegetical practice today.

> He did not want to *glorify* his own name, he did not want to build a monument to himself with his work but rather truly to serve the Gospel, *to create an ecclesial theology, neither individual nor based on himself.* . . . Actually, he succeeded in elaborating a . . . "de-individualized" theology, that is, a theology which expresses a common thought and language.[6]

Of course, we might apply these same words to the theological project of Joseph Ratzinger, Pope Benedict XVI. But he seems here to be trying to make a broader, almost methodological statement. True theology must always be in the service of the gospel, which is the Word that gathers the Church in adoration in every generation. It must seek not to give voice to one's own personal opinions[7] but to be a mouthpiece for the authentic Word of Christ. Hence it must also be *an ecclesial theology.*

The exegete and theologian must read with passion and with the eye of a scholar. The Scriptures, as we have said so often in the previous pages, are intended to be more than informative. They are meant to be performative, transformative, and life changing. The aim of the written text is to become living Word in the heart of the believer. Our study of the Scriptures, then, must not be a search for knowledge only. We must also read to refresh and renew

5. *Jesus*, 35–36. See also *Way*, 91–92; *Song*, 30: "Perhaps this is actually the origin of the word 'antichrist': to be against Jesus as the Christ, to deny him the predicate 'Christ.'" Cf. 1 John 2:18, 22; 4:3.

6. Pope Benedict XVI, General Audience (May 14, 2008); emphasis added.

7. *Theology*, 93–96.

our souls, and our theology must seek to bring refreshment and renewal to others' souls as well.

In this light, we can understand Benedict's frequent exhortations as pope concerning the need to retrieve the ancient practice of *lectio divina*, the loving contemplation of Scripture in which study is transformed into prayer. Indeed, Benedict has gone so far as to say that the widespread adoption of *lectio divina* would bring to the Church "a new springtime."[8] He has even given this advice to the highest officials in the Church, those ultimately entrusted with the sacred duty of providing binding interpretations of the divine Word. In one of his first addresses as pope, he urged the world's bishops: "We must practice '*Lectio divina*.' We must grasp Christ's way of thinking in the Scriptures, we must learn to think with Christ, to think Christ's thoughts and thus feel Christ's sentiments, to be able to convey Christ's thinking to others."[9]

This could almost serve as a mission statement for those of us in the guild of professional theology and exegesis. Our use of reason and reflection must always go hand-in-hand with prayer, which is the dialogue of the believer who seeks, through the illumination of the Holy Spirit, to hear the voice of the living God in the sacred text. Benedict once again points us to the early Church for our model. We have a good description of the unity of faith and reason, prayer and study, in his description of Origen's method:

> Notwithstanding all the theological richness of his thought, his is never a purely academic approach; it is always founded on the experience of prayer, of contact with God. Indeed, to his mind, knowledge of the Scriptures requires prayer and intimacy with Christ even more than study. He was convinced that the best way to become acquainted with God is through love, and that there is no authentic *scientia Christi* without falling in love with him.[10]

8. Pope Benedict XVI, Address to the Participants in the International Congress Organized to Commemorate the Fortieth Anniversary of the Dogmatic Constitution on Divine Revelation, *Dei Verbum* (September 16, 2005).

9. Pope Benedict XVI, Reflection on the Opening of the Eleventh Ordinary General Assembly of the Synod of Bishops (October 3, 2005), in *L'Osservatore Romano*, Weekly Edition in English (October 12, 2005), 7.

10. Pope Benedict XVI, General Audience (May 2, 2007).

The key, always, is to approach our task with humility.

> Intellectual humility is the primary rule for one who searches to
> penetrate the supernatural realities beginning from the sacred Book.
> Obviously, humility does not exclude serious study; but to ensure
> that the results are spiritually beneficial, facilitating true entry into
> the depth of the text, humility remains indispensable. Only with
> this interior attitude can one really listen to and eventually perceive
> the voice of God. On the other hand, when it is a question of the
> Word of God, understanding it means nothing if it does not lead
> to action.[11]

Pride goes before the fall into error and sometimes even into
apostasy. The pope points to the cautionary case of Tertullian, the
second-century Church Father who in his pride ended up dying in
schism. It is hard not to hear echoes of the present day in Benedict's
reading of this sad case, and we are reminded, too, that in addition to being a great theologian, Benedict is also a wise confessor
and pastor of souls:

> One sees that in the end he [Tertullian] lacked the simplicity, the
> humility to integrate himself with the Church, to accept his weak-
> nesses, to be forbearing with others and himself. When one only
> sees his thought in all its greatness, in the end, it is precisely this
> greatness that is lost. *The essential characteristic of a great theolo-*
> *gian is the humility to remain with the Church*, to accept his own
> and others' weaknesses, because actually only God is all holy. We,
> instead, always need forgiveness.[12]

Real Progress in Theological Understanding

Humility, prayer, and a faith that works in love, seeking the Christ
who calls us—these are the essential characteristics of authentic
scientia Christi, as Benedict proposes it to us. "We have to enter
into a relationship of awe and obedience toward the Bible. . . .

---

11. Pope Benedict XVI, General Audience (June 4, 2008).
12. Pope Benedict XVI, General Audience (May 30, 2007); emphasis added.

Historical-critical exegesis can be a wonderful means for a deeper understanding of the Bible if its instruments are used with that reverent love which seeks to know God's gift in the most exact and careful way possible."[13]

An exegesis and theology borne of humility is always open to new discoveries, to the experience of the great saints and doctors of the Church who understood the Word to be unfathomable in its riches yet disclosing itself the more one seeks understanding in faith, hope, and love. Quoting the dictum of the medieval writer Richard of St. Victor, "Love is the faculty of seeing," Benedict reminds us that "all real progress in theological understanding has its origin in the eye of love and in its faculty of beholding."[14] And he promises the theologian that reading in continuity with this ecclesial tradition "increases the excitement and fecundity of inquiry."

> How exciting exegesis becomes when it dares to read the Bible as a unified whole. If the Bible originates from the one subject formed by the people of God and, through it, from the divine subject himself, then it speaks of the present. If this is so, moreover, even what we know about the diversity of its underlying historical constellations yields its harvest; there is a unity to be discovered in this diversity, and diversity appears as the wealth of unity. This opens up a wide field of action both to historical research and to its hypotheses, with the sole limit that it may not destroy the unity of the whole, which is situated on another plane than what can be called the "nuts and bolts" of the various texts. Unity is found on another plane, yet it belongs to the literary reality of the Bible itself.[15]

Therefore, exegesis, the true reading of Holy Scripture, is not only a literary phenomenon, not only reading a text. It is the movement of my existence. It is moving towards the Word of God in the human words. Only by conforming ourselves to the mystery of God, to the Lord who is the Word, can we enter within the Word, can we truly find the Word of God in human words. Let us pray to the Lord

13. *Song*, 50. See also *Theology*, 97.
14. *Pierced*, 27.
15. *Theology*, 64–65.

that he may help us search the word, not only with our intellect but also with our entire existence.[16]

Benedict, then, presents us with a vision of a profound spiritual and scientific exegesis: a faith, in conversation with the living God, seeking understanding of the deepest mysteries of the cosmos. For the theologian and exegete of faith, the work of theology and exegesis assumes a place within the grand unity of God's plan as it is revealed in Scripture, namely, that of bringing about the "divinization" of creation in the liturgical offering of the sacrifice of praise.

> The unity of the person of Jesus, embracing man and God, prefig-
> ures that synthesis of man and world to which theology is meant
> to minister. It is my belief that the beauty and necessity of the
> theologian's task could be made visible at this point. . . . But [the
> theologian] can only do this provided he himself enters that "labora-
> tory" of unity and freedom . . . where his own will is refashioned,
> where he allows himself to be expropriated and inserted into the
> divine will, where he advances toward that God-likeness through
> which the kingdom of God can come.[17]

And if we take Benedict's thought seriously and consider the New Testament authors to be the normative theologians, then our study of Scripture will bring us into the heart of what might be called the sacerdotal nature of the biblical texts.

Let us close, then, with a particularly fertile passage, one that indicates the beauty and necessity of the theological and exegetical task, as well as the excitement and fecundity of Benedict's own research. Through a close reading of the text, he notes the curious preponderance of cultic and priestly language in Romans 15:16, where Paul describes his purpose in writing his letter as part of his mission "to be a minister of Christ Jesus to the Gentiles in the priestly service of the gospel of God, so that the offering of the Gentiles may be acceptable."

16. Meditation during the First General Congregation of the 12th Ordinary General Assembly of the Synod of Bishops (October 6, 2008).

17. *Pierced*, 46. See also *Liturgy*, 28.

The Letter to the Romans, this word that has been written that it may then be proclaimed, is an apostolic action; more, it is a liturgical—even a cultic—event. This it is because it helps the world of the pagans to change so as to be a renewal of mankind and, as such, a cosmic liturgy in which mankind shall become adoration, become the radiance of the glory of God. If the apostle is handing on the Gospel by means of this letter, this is not a matter of religious or philosophical propaganda, nor is it a social mission or even a personal and charismatic enterprise. . . . *This is a priestly sacrificial action, an eschatological service of ministry*: the fulfillment and the perfecting of the Old Testament sacrificial services. In this verse Paul presents himself . . . "as sacrificial priest of the eschatological cosmos."

If, in the Letter to the Philippians, we found martyrdom being presented as a liturgical event, associated with the theology of the cross and with eucharistic theology; if, in Romans 12, the same was being said to us about the Christian life as such; now it is the specifically apostolic service of preaching the faith that appears as a priestly activity, as actually performing the new liturgy, open to all the world and likewise worldwide, which has been founded by . . . the *pascha* of Jesus Christ and . . . his presence in the Church through the Eucharist.[18]

Here Benedict opens wide a new window into the scriptural text, one in which we see the unity of the Old and New Testaments, of Church and Scripture, Word and sacrament, the Bible and the liturgy—a unity in service of the divine plan, which is a participation in the mystery of God. This beautiful verse of St. Paul defines the mission of the biblical theologian: to become a true liturgist of Jesus Christ, to help prepare the world to become the cosmic liturgy it was meant to be in the beginning. And this is the mission that Benedict has given himself.

In this verse [Rom. 15:16] alone does Paul use the word *hierourgein*—to administer as a priest—together with *leitourgos*, liturgy: he speaks of the cosmic liturgy in which the human world itself must become worship of God, an oblation in the Holy Spirit. When

18. *Pilgrim*, 118–19; emphasis added.

the world in all its parts has become a liturgy of God, when, in its reality, it has become adoration, then it will have reached its goal and will be safe and sound. This is the ultimate goal of St. Paul's apostolic mission as well as of our own mission. The Lord calls us to this ministry. Let us pray at this time that he may help us to carry it out properly—to become true liturgists of Jesus Christ.[19]

19. Pope Benedict XVI, Homily, Eucharistic Concelebration on the Solemnity of the Holy Apostles Peter and Paul (June 29, 2008).

Scripture Index

Genesis

1:1–2:4 139
2:21–22 LXX 164
3:1–7 121n28, 170
4:4 158
11:1–9 131
12:1–3 123n32
12:2–3 102n35
22:2 158
22:8 158
22:13 158
22:17–18 128n56

Exodus

3:13 143n24
3:14 60
3:15–16 143n24
4:22 127
12:23 150
19:16–19 130
24:6 150, 151
24:8 150, 151

Leviticus

8:3 143n20

2 Samuel

7:11–16 132
7:12–13 127
23:5 132

1 Kings

12:31 129n61
13:33 129n61

2 Chronicles

3:1 158

Psalms

22 144, 171
23 152n51
40:1–12 171n25
40:6 166
40:6–8 156
50:8–14 155n59
50:12–13 155
51 171n25
51:16–17 155n59
69 171n25
69:30–31 155n59
89 132

118 22
119:108 155n59

Isaiah

2:3 102n35
11:12 127n54
13:4 127n54
25:6–9 184n65
45:23 99
53 150
62:10 102n35

Jeremiah

3:17 127n54
23:3 127n54
31:31–34 150

Ezekiel

34 26n4
34:13 127n54
34:23 127n54

Zechariah

9:12 102n35

197

Matthew

10:7–9 49n16
10:39 120
10:40 49n16
11:25 128n59
12:30 127
16:18–19 128
24:27 182n60
26:17–20 147n41
26:28 150
27:16 134n79
28:20 51

Mark

1:22 80
3:14 129, 129n61
3:14–19 49n16
8:35 120
9:4 144n25
10:24 128n59
14:12–17 147n41
14:24 129, 150

Luke

9:31 144
10:16 49n16
22:7–16 147n41
22:14–20 139
22:20 150
23:19 134n79
23:25 134n79
24:25–31 175
24:27 80, 101n28
24:35 141
24:44–45 101n28

John

1:29 148
2:21 80
2:22 79
4:22 102n35, 132
4:24 72
7:38 52n30
11:52 127
12:28 173

12:32 166
14:26 79
14:28 160
16:12 53
16:13 112n68
17:21 173
18:40 134n79
19:14 147n41
19:34 52n30, 164
19:37 170n21
20:21 49n16

Acts

1:6 134
1:8 131, 131n68
2 130
2:5 130
2:42 54, 141
16:6–10 38
28:30–31 131

Romans

6:17 56
8:15–16 145n32
10:9 57
12 179n48, 195
12:1 178
15:16 194, 195

1 Corinthians

6:7 166
10:1–4 140n9
11:23–26 139
11:25 150, 152n51
11:26 56
15:28 120, 139, 167, 179,
      181, 185
16:22 183n61, 185

2 Corinthians

3 109
3:6–18 52n27
3:17 109
10:10 182n60

Galatians

3:28 166
4:6 145n32
4:26 137

Ephesians

1:10 138
2:19–22 52n30
3:8–11 138

Philippians

2:5–11 123
2:6–11 98
2:12 182n60

Hebrews

1:1–2 66
2:15 121n28, 170
10:5 166
10:5–7 156
10:20 160
12:18–24 130

1 Peter

3:15 67, 74
3:20–21 140n9

1 John

2:18 190n5
2:22 190n5
4:3 190n5
4:7–8 138
4:8 170n21

3 John

8 16

Revelation

19:7–9 184n65
21:6 52n30
21:9–14 52n30
22:1 52n30
22:17 52n30, 185
22:20 183n61, 185

Subject Index

Aaron, 142
Abel, 158
Abraham
  call of, 122
  faithfulness of, 174
  Jesus' lineage to, 124
  sacrifice of Isaac, 158, 164
Abrahamic covenant, 123, 128
academic study, as worship, 188
Adam, 124
allegorism, 35–36
already and not yet, 123n32, 138
ancient Near Eastern treaties, 117
Anthony, 176
antichrists, 189
apologetics, 67, 68
apostles, 49, 128, 129
apostolic succession, 47–50, 54, 56, 61, 66
Aristotle, 87
atonement, 154, 163
Augustine, 17n9, 18, 68, 111, 189
authority of mystery, 22
autonomy, 128n59

Balthasar, Hans Urs von, 17, 19, 89
baptism, 53, 57, 58, 140, 165, 169, 177
Barabbas, 134
Benedict, 118
Benedict XVI, Pope

and biblical theology, 13–14, 23–24
  career of, 18–19
  ecclesiology of, 64–65
  election as pope, 13
  encounter with historical-critical
    method, 19–20
  preaching of, 148
  on Mary, 133
  Word-centeredness of, 48–50, 56
  writings of, 15–17
Berakah, 178
Bible. See Scripture
biblical theology, 13–14, 23–24, 62, 91
  and covenant, 116
  as liturgy, 195
  and systematic theology, 43–44
  and unity of Bible, 100–102
blessing, 178
blood of the covenant, 129, 149–54
body of Christ, 142
Bonaventure, 17n9, 67, 87, 110
Bultmann, Rudolph, 32

canon, 47–49, 53, 61, 78–79, 100
catechesis, 58, 61, 68
Catechism of the Catholic Church, 19,
    97
catholicity, of Church, 131, 138, 145
chalice, 152n51

Christ
  as interpretive key of Scriptures, 91
  pierced side of, 164–65, 180
Christian life, 169
Christology, 15, 72, 97–99, 124–25, 143–44
Church
  as a gathering together, 64
  apostolic structure of, 48
  authority of, 70
  and Bible, 21, 46–50, 78
  as body of Christ, 165, 166
  as *communio*, 141–42, 166
  and exegesis, 31–32, 42, 44
  as family of God, 116, 128, 132
  as inner goal of creation, 137
  and Israel, 135–36
  and kingdom, 125–28, 135
  as living subject of theology, 75–77, 79
  as living transmission of faith, 69
  as living voice, 50
  as memory, 50, 80
  mission of, 53, 55–56, 166
  as new Israel, 137
  as new *qahal*, 130
  subsists in liturgy, 141–42
  as temple of God, 52
  and tradition, 52–53
  and the Word, 53, 54–57
Communio (journal), 19
comparative religion, 183
confession of faith, 29–30, 58–59
consanguinity, between God and humanity, 153n51
contemplation, 89
"contemporaneity with Christ," 55
conversion, 58, 61, 73–74
"cooperators in the truth," 16
cosmic liturgy, 164, 181–85, 195–96
Council of Chalcedon, 98n19
Council of Nicaea, 59–60
covenant, 55, 101–2, 116–17, 136, 139
  in creation, 118
  renewal of, 142
creation, 118, 121, 187
Creed, 54, 58–60
cross
  and Eucharist, 148–49, 154
  and salvation history, 159–61, 163

crucifixion, 124
  as cosmic liturgy, 164
Cyril of Jerusalem, 111, 142

Davidic kingdom, 122, 123, 127, 132–35
Day of Atonement, 149, 157n63
Dead Sea Scrolls, 147
death, victory over, 168–72, 173
de-Hellenization, of Christianity, 28,
  36–39, 56
Dei Verbum, 14, 18, 95n10
dialogue, of Church and Word, 65, 66–68
Dibelius, Martin, 32
discipleship, 73
divine economy, 115–16, 135, 140
divine pedagogy, 116
divinization, 120–21, 139, 154

early Church, 191
Eastern Fathers of the Church, 120
ecclesial tradition, 30
ecclesiology, eucharistic, 141–42
Emmaus narrative, 80, 82, 175
Enlightenment, 31–32
epistemological agnosticism, 32
eschatology, 169
Essenes, 147
eternal life, 187
Eucharist, 53, 54, 138–42, 165
  and cross, 148-49, 154
  as feast of new creation, 169
  as fulfillment of old covenant liturgies,
    105, 167–68
  as heart of new covenant, 129
  and Passover, 48, 105
Eucharistic Prayer, 172, 177–81
Eunomius, 30
evolution, 28–30, 34, 42
exegesis, 26, 41, 94, 95–96, 110
  and theology, 43–44
exile, 150, 155
Exodus, 122, 140, 144, 160, 161
expiation, 154, 158
ex-sistere, 160

faith
  of the Church, 78
  and history, 96
  and knowledge, 45–46

and reason, 32, 34, 36–38, 44, 73, 74,
    83–86, 92, 96–97, 108, 191, 194
and revelation, 109–10
seeking understanding, 70, 85
fall, 121, 154
family of God, 116, 128, 132
Fathers of the Church, 16, 77, 83, 94, 111,
    140, 158, 177
fellowship, 141–42
form criticism, 46
Francis of Assisi, 176

gathering, of children of God, 127
gnosticism, 96
God
    dialogue with, 119, 146
    as Father, 146
    love of, 170
    self-revelation, 88, 90
    as Spirit, 72
    as subject of theology, 87–88
Good Samaritan, 124
Gospels, 98
    Jewish elements in, 28–29
Greek language, 38–39
Greek philosophy, 28–29, 82–83, 87, 179
Gregory of Nyssa, 30–31
Gregory the Great, 13
Guardini, Romano, 93

Haggadah, 178
Harnack, Adolf von, 21n26
Heim, Maximilian Heinrich, 14n3
Heisenberg principle, 28
Hellenization, 155, 178
hermeneutic(s)
    christological, 79
    of continuity, 188
    of faith, 42, 60–62, 79, 92, 93–94, 95–97,
        101, 161
    secular, 43
    of suspicion, 30, 42
Hesiod, 87
historical-critical method, 19–20, 25–40,
    41–42, 44, 47, 61, 62, 63, 69, 78, 98,
    105, 107–8, 125, 149, 182–83, 193
historical facticity, 97, 104–5
historicism, 78

history, 25, 34
homoousios, 59–60
hope, 133, 185
human personhood, and Incarnation, 65
humility, 190, 192, 193
hypotheses, exegesis as, 42

Incarnation, 65–66
inner Word, 67
inspiration, 103–4
International Theological Commission, 19
interpretation, 41–45, 51–52, 69, 94, 113
Irenaeus, 116
Isaac, 158, 164, 177
Israel, and the Church, 48, 135–36

Jeremiah, on new covenant, 150–51
Jerome, 20
Jesus
    and Church, 66
    death of, 72, 144–45
    genealogies of, 124, 133-34
    as Lamb, 148, 159, 164
    as new temple, 148, 165–66
    participation in liturgy, 144
    prayer of, 143–46
    preaching of, 80–82, 125–26, 134
    resurrection of, 36, 72, 81
    sacrifice of, 151, 154-56, 163–64
    speech as sacramental, 174
    as summary of Christian confession, 59
    as "true David", 133
Jesus of Nazareth (Benedict XVI), 14–15,
    20, 29, 124
Jews, 102, 132
John, Gospel of, 26, 147-48
John Chrysostom, 169
John Paul II, Pope, 23

Kant, Immanuel, 32, 37, 84
keys of the kingdom, 128
kingdom of God, 55, 184–85
    and Church, 125–28, 135
    and Davidic kingdom, 134–35
knowledge, and faith, 45–46
koinonia, 94, 141–42

Lamb, 158–59
language, multidimensional nature of, 104

last days, 123n32, 138
Last Supper, 124, 145, 147–54, 170–71
law, 119–20
Law and Gospel, 123
lectio divina, 89, 191
Leo the Great, 175
liberal theology, 37
listening, hermeneutic of faith as, 45
literalism, 37
literal meaning, 102–5
literary methods, 44
liturgical ecclesiology, 131
liturgical order, 119
liturgy, 93, 99n23, 137–42, 195–96
  as actualization of Scripture's truths, 91
  centrality of, 54
  and dogma, 18
  as goal of creation, 181
  as *opus Dei*, 146, 147
  and Word, 112–13
Liturgy of the Word, 176
Logos, 29, 39, 65, 67, 84, 86, 178–79, 181
Loisy, Alfred, 125, 135
Lord's Day, 168–69
lordship of God, 126–27
Lord's Prayer, 146, 184–85
love, 67–68, 193
Lubac, Henri de, 19
Luther, Martin, 37, 75, 123

Maier, Friedrich Wilhelm, 27n6
manna, 184
Maranatha, 185
Mary, 133, 175
Mass, 112, 145, 168, 172–81
memoria ecclesiae, 50, 80
Messiah, 59, 123, 124, 132, 133
metaphysics, 84, 180
miracles, 33, 149
modern exegesis, 29, 61
modern reason, 84–85
Monod, Jacques, 33
moral order, 119
Munich, 16–17
mystagogy, 61, 140
mystery, of the Word, 22

narrative ecclesiology, 131
natural science, 37

natural sciences, 28–29, 108
  objectivity of, 33
nature, 85
Neusner, Jacob, 101
new Adam, 165, 180
new covenant, 51, 101, 109, 117, 122, 129, 130, 138, 150–53
  worship, 166–68
new creation, 164, 167, 169, 180
new Israel, 128
new Jerusalem, 185
new song, 171
New Testament
  relation to Old Testament, 111
  trustworthiness of, 98
normative theologians, 71–72, 75, 77, 79, 81, 86–87, 90, 94, 174, 194
normativity, 94

oikonomia, 115
old covenant, 51, 109, 117, 122, 127, 150, 167
Old Testament, 51, 122
  christological interpretation of, 111
  and covenant, 117
  sacrifices of, 156–57, 158
"ontological precedence of the Church," 137
opus Dei, liturgy as, 146, 147
oratio, 145, 172, 177, 178
Origen, 191
original sin, 154

parousia, 182–83
paschal mystery, 138–39, 157–58, 159, 171
Pascher, Joseph, 93
Passover, 48, 105, 147, 149, 160, 164
patriarchs, 144
Pentecost, 130
performative, Word as, 66, 140, 174
personhood, and dialogue, 119n17
Peter, as rock, 128
physiologein, 31
pilgrimage, 184–85
Pius XI, Pope, 102
Plato, 188
Pontifical Biblical Commission, 19
positivist hermeneutics, 43

"postulate of objectivity," 33
prayer, 89, 93, 113, 143–46, 190, 191
preaching, 68, 70–71
pride, 192
priesthood, 56, 142, 167
primitive Christianity, 63–64
Prodigal Son, 124
progress, in theology, 192–94
prophets, 133, 150–51
propitiation, 154
Pseudo-Dionysius, 87, 190

qahal, 129–30, 142, 144, 171

Rahner, Karl, 17
Ratzinger, Joseph Cardinal. See Benedict
    XVI, Pope
reason, 37–40, 84–85. See also faith, and
    reason
reconciliation, 127n53
redaction criticism, 46
Reformation, 37
regula fidei. See rule of faith
Reimarus, Hermann, 31n15
renewal movements, 14
ressourcement, 64
resurrection, 42–43, 159–61, 169
revelation, 95n10
    and faith, 109–10
    and history, 25
    and human response, 65
    as living organism, 77
    and theology, 66–67
Revelation (book of), 182
Richard of St. Victor, 193
road to Emmaus. See Emmaus narrative
Rome, 131
Rowland, Tracey, 14n3
rule of faith (regula fidei), 47–49, 53, 61,
    110

Sabbath, 118, 119
sacramental mysticism, 181
sacraments, 48, 52, 53, 57, 66
    as actualization of Word, 55
    and salvation history, 140
sacrifice, 150, 151, 163
    transformation of, 154–56, 178, 179

sacrifice of praise, 178, 194
salvation history, 56, 115, 138, 187
    and cross and resurrection, 159–61
    and sacraments, 140
    teleology of, 153
    unity of, 176–77
Scheeban, Matthias, 16
schism, 192
Schmaus, Michael, 93
science, 28, 62, 63
scientia Christi, 192
scientific exegesis, 31–32, 51, 194
"scientific theology," 71
Scripture
    and Church, 35, 46–50, 78, 82
    coherent story of, 115
    and Eucharist, 175
    reliability of, 72, 74
    sacerdotal nature of, 194
    senses of, 102–5, 106–7, 109
    "subjectivizing" of, 36
    and Tradition, 75
    unity of, 78–79, 91, 100–102, 122
Second Vatican Council, 14, 18, 50, 95n10,
    100n24, 141n15
secular academy, 188
Septuagint, 38
servant songs of Isaiah, 133, 150
service, 65
sin, 121
Sinai, as archetype of Church, 142
Sinai covenant, 122, 123, 129, 149, 151,
    153
Söhngen, Gottlieb, 93
sola Scriptura, 37, 76
Soloviev, Vladimir, 189
Son of God, 127, 157
Son of Man, 133
source criticism, 103
speech-act, 173-74, 180
spiritual exegesis, 14, 110, 161
spiritual science, 71–73
spiritual sense, of Scripture, 107, 108–9
spiritual worship, 156, 178–79
subsistit, 141n15
substitution, 154–56, 157n63
succession. See apostolic succession
"surplus" of meaning, 104–5

symbol, 29
symphonic relationship, between Testaments, 111
Synod of Bishops (2008), 189
systematic theology, 43, 92

tabernacle, 118
technology, 37, 39
Temple, 52, 148, 165–66
Tertullian, 192
testament of God, 116, 117. *See also* covenant
theiosis, 120–21, 139
theología, 87
theologichē, 87
theology
   and dogmas of Church, 71
   as ecclesial, 69–70, 75, 188, 190
   engagement with philosophy and sciences, 83
   and exegesis, 43–44
   and God's self-revelation, 88
   as interpretation, 69
   presupposes faith, 66
   as spiritual science, 71–73, 75, 82, 84
   vs. economy, 115
theophany, 169

"third day," 169
Thomas Aquinas, 16
todah psalms, 171–72
tower of Babel, 131
Tradition, 49, 50–53, 75
transubstantiation, 180, 185
Trinity, 139, 146
truth, 16–17
twelve, 129, 130–31
typology, 108–13, 115, 124–25, 164–65, 176–77

University of Munich, 18
University of Tübingen, 18

verbal sacrifice, 156

water and blood, 165
wedding feast, 152n51
Weigel, George, 23
Word and event, 107–8
world, as temple-kingdom of God, 119
worship, 65, 88, 93, 99n23, 112, 118, 119–20, 142, 146

Zealots, 134
Zion, 127, 133